JOB HUNTING
THE NEW RULES

JOB HUNTING
THE NEW RULES

DR ROB YEUNG

Marshall Cavendish
Business

Copyright © 2009 Rob Yeung

This paperback edition published in 2009 by

Marshall Cavendish Limited
Fifth Floor
32–38 Saffron Hill
London EC1N 8FH
United Kingdom
T: +44 (0)20 7421 8120
F: +44 (0)20 7421 8121
sales@marshallcavendish.co.uk
www.marshallcavendish.co.uk

First hardback edition published in 2006 as *The Rules of Job Hunting*

The right of Rob Yeung to be identified as the author of this work has been asserted
by him in accordance with the Copyright, Designs and Patents Act 1988.

A CIP record for this book is available from the British Library

ISBN 978-0-462-09928-6

Designed by Robert Jones
Project managed by Cambridge Publishing Management Ltd

Printed and bound in Great Britain by
CPI Bookmarque, Croydon CR0 4TD

CONTENTS

FOREWORD

Working life ain't simple any more. There was a time when you worked hard, your employer looked after you, and you just carried on until you received your gold carriage clock on retirement. But that simple career path is dead. There are more threats in the world—mergers and acquisitions, globalization and jobs being outsourced or offshored, downsizing programs, and job cuts. And these have turned the workplace into a minefield of treacherous personalities, unexploded resentments, and ticking egos. Whom can you really trust? What do you need to do or say to get ahead? And what exactly are employers looking for?

But there are more opportunities too. You aren't tied to the one organization any more—you can move around and seek bigger pay rises, greater responsibility, more interesting challenges. Employers no longer look down on people who want to take career breaks to go traveling or do something different. You can go freelance or set up your own business and try to make your first million. The world is your oyster.

In this complex world of work, the rules of work have changed. We can all think of people who got promoted who didn't deserve to. Come to think of it, we can all probably think of someone who does deserve to get promoted, but hasn't been. And, to add insult to injury, on top of our day-to-day jobs, we're expected to deal with office politics, to be a good leader and team player, and to network. And how do you get headhunted exactly? All of these are things that no one ever really tells you how to do.

Well, this series tells you how to do these things. And this book looks at the rules of job-hunting.

It used to be the case that you listed your education and experience on a CV and sent it off to employers. If you were lucky, they would invite you in for an interview and select the most skilled candidate. But the rules of the game have changed. A big chunk of jobs are never advertised but filled through word of mouth. CVs can take innumerable forms to show off your best attributes and hide your weak spots. And interviewers have new, devious tools and techniques to put you under pressure. So this book is filled with insider advice and tips to help you track down and secure the right job for you.

But let's cut to the chase. After all, who has the time to sit and read hefty management tomes? Too often, an author has a handful of great ideas, but then ruins it by spending hundreds and hundreds of pages explaining it carefully in excruciating detail, giving too much background and yawn yawn yawn ... I've lost the will to live.

When I read one of those books, I start to flick through the chapters and pages with increasing impatience—wanting to shout, "Come On, Get To The Point!" Ah, but there is a reason why so many books are so long. Many publishers want their authors to write lengthy books so that they can slap on a big fat cover price. So this book is short and full of practical, pithy advice in bite-sized chunks.

If you want to know how to nail the right job—but don't have the time to plow through Bible-sized manuals or books that talk down to you—then this is the book for you.

Finally, if you have any odd experiences or job-hunting tips—drop me an email. I'll shove it in the next edition and you'll get your name in print!

Rob Yeung
rob@talentspace.co.uk

INTRODUCTION

If you consider the whole job-hunting process, it would seem at a first glance that the rules of job-hunting haven't really changed that much over the years. You still put together a CV listing your skills and experience; perhaps you try to mention a few interesting hobbies or interests to grab the recruiter's attention. You still submit your CV to an employer or perhaps through a third-party recruitment consultancy or executive search firm. And if you are lucky, you are still invited to interview. Yes, it all looks pretty familiar so far, doesn't it?

But while it all looks safe and familiar on the surface, the reality is that job-hunting has actually changed hugely in recent years as a result of increasing competition between organizations to reduce costs. More and more organizations are trying to offload employees by restructuring, downsizing, offshoring, and outsourcing. More and more jobs are being handed to contractors, consultants, and other temporary staff. And for the employees that remain, they are being asked to be more adaptable and hard-working. After all, the same (if not more) work needs to be done—just by fewer people.

All of this has meant that organizations have got that much more careful about hiring people. Human resources departments and line managers are now much more canny at screening candidates and putting them through many more challenging tests and interviews to choose the very best.

As a business psychologist, I am hired by organizations to help with their recruitment and interviewing programs. And having interviewed hundreds of candidates and designed dozens of assessment centers in organizations ranging from international investment banks and law firms to airlines, insurers, and transport companies, I am going to share with you some of the unspoken rules and guerrilla tactics that will capitalize on your strengths and boost your chances at every stage of the job-hunting process. I've split the book into five parts:

- *Understanding the product.* Your first step is to understand the product that is you. What do you really want out of your career? What can you bring to a new employer? And what are the limitations and personal flaws that could scupper your chances? Identifying your goals and aspirations, strengths and weaknesses, will enable you to focus on the right opportunities for you and present yourself in the most favorable light to interviewers.
- *Creating a winning CV.* At first glance, writing a CV seems to be the most straightforward part of job-hunting. But too many CVs actually betray all sorts of reasons why recruiters should not invite the candidates to interview. Make sure that you understand the new rules and unspoken truths of CV writing to ensure that you highlight your strengths and bury your weaknesses.
- *Opening up opportunities.* There's a huge "hidden market" of jobs that are never advertised. A lot of employers fill vacancies by alternative tactics,

including the use of headhunters and agencies, speculative applications, word of mouth, and approaching people they already know. Using your research and networking skills will open up a surprising number of opportunities that you might otherwise never come across.

- *Being unforgettable at interviews.* I've interviewed hundreds of managers and it always amazes me that great managers often make terrible interview candidates. Make sure that you know how to present yourself in the best possible light to see off the competition.
- *Signing on the dotted line.* Nearly there, the final few feet to the finishing line—it's a great feeling to be offered a job. But before you sign on the dotted line, how can you get the best possible deal and make sure that the job really is the right one for you?

Job-hunting is often described as a full-time job in itself. And it certainly needs hard work and discipline to chase leads and fend off the competition. So let's get started.

UNDERSTANDING
THE PRODUCT

It doesn't take a genius to appreciate that a job search is essentially a marketing campaign. There's a product to promote (i.e. you). There are customers—otherwise known as employers. And there is a marketplace, in which many, many other products (other candidates) are competing with your product for attention. Taking the analogy a little further, you need to take steps to advertise and raise customers' awareness of the features, benefits, and reasons to buy your particular product. Of course, what you really want is for a horde of customers to queue up and fight over your product.

But a lot of job-hunters try to run before they can walk. They miss a vital first step and jump straight to step two—writing or rewriting their CV. But that really isn't the place to start. Do marketers jump in and throw their resources at an advertising campaign without understanding what their product does? No, of course not.

Like any product, you have particular features and benefits. But you might have limitations or flaws too. And when a product is really good, it's often the case that some customers simply won't be able to afford it—some candidates automatically scupper their chances by being overqualified or too highly paid. Nothing is ever perfect in the world of product marketing. So let's work through this first step toward launching your marketing campaign by understanding the precise features and benefits, strengths and weaknesses of the very idiosyncratic product that is you.

SCRUTINIZE YOURSELF

I was presenting at a conference recently and I asked the members of the audience to raise their hands if they thought they were better-than-average drivers. About two-thirds of the room put their hands in the air. Then I asked if they thought they had better-than-average senses of humor. This time, about three-quarters of the audience lifted their hands into the air. Finally, I asked them to raise their hands if they thought they were above-average lovers. With a ripple of amusement, a veritable sea of hands filled the air.

The fact is that nearly everyone thinks they are better than average and hardly anyone thinks they are below par at anything.

Most people deceive themselves to some degree about their own strengths and weaknesses. It's a built-in defense mechanism that all humans have— for the most part our brains choose to overlook our failings and limitations because it protects our self-esteem.

But of course understanding your true strengths and weaknesses has important implications for your job search.

So I dare you to scrutinize your strengths and weaknesses as objectively and harshly as you can. Be as honest and unsympathetic as you can. Jot down a list of ten or so major skills or key strengths. Do it. Don't just skip ahead, believing yourself to be above the need for such introspection. Get a pen and scribble a couple of notes in the column of this book if need be. And then write down an equal number of personal flaws and weaknesses.

SEE YOURSELF AS OTHERS SEE YOU

I know a freelance human resources consultant who is trying to get a job back in the world of the large corporates because she's having trouble making ends meet as a freelancer. She is well spoken and intelligent, hard-working and professional. Unfortunately, she will never get a job in a big corporate until she realizes that she comes across as defeatist and totally lacking in drive.

Identifying what you think are your strengths and weaknesses is only a start. Because the hard work comes in finding out how you come across to others. Perceptions are very subtle, and others often see slightly more or slightly less of our strengths than we might believe.

Just think. You might think that you're quite confident, but employers might see you as slightly too confident—bordering on arrogant—or even insecure and less confident than you believe. Or you might see yourself as being quite ambitious, while employers could see you as being ambitious to the point of ruthlessness—or perhaps insufficiently ambitious and actually a bit of a doormat.

Such gaps between your self-perception and how others perceive you could put you at a disadvantage in your job search. Headhunters or consultants might put you forward for jobs at the wrong sorts of companies. And interviewers might turn you down because they simply can't see you fitting into their cultures.

Most job-hunters benefit from soliciting feedback from people who know them. You may have engaged in similar exercises on management development programs, so I won't dwell on the detail. How you go about seeking feedback is up to you. Some job-hunters prefer to email a short explanation and a handful of open-ended questions to acquaintances and contacts; others prefer to warn contacts by email and then follow up with a telephone conversation. Just make sure you do it.

TEAR YOURSELF APART

No one likes to be slapped in the face. But if you want to gather useful feedback, then that's effectively what you need to ask your contacts to do to you. Few people are sufficiently critical of themselves. Asking for feedback should be at least a slightly uncomfortable exercise for you. If you are not at least slightly surprised or disappointed by the feedback, you have probably not approached the right people or asked for it in the right way.

Resist asking family and intimate friends as they may not know how you come across in a business context and in any case they may be too close to you to be able to offer you objective feedback. They would rather offer feedback that equates to a metaphorical hug than a slap in the face. Business acquaintances such as colleagues, clients, and suppliers may be able to provide you with more useful feedback in relation to how recruiters and interviewers might perceive you. But do think about whom to pick, as some colleagues might be tempted to gossip about your attempts to gather feedback.

What you ask is often less important than how you ask it. A lot of job-hunters say that respondents are reluctant to give candid feedback. Respondents tend to feel more comfortable giving positive strokes than negative feedback. So encourage respondents to be as honest as they can. Emphasize that no one is perfect and remind them that the feedback will help you in your personal development. If they list three strengths for you, encourage them to identify three weaknesses to provide you with a balanced picture.

But the golden rule of soliciting feedback is to avoid becoming defensive. Remember that your respondents are trying to help you by being honest with you. And they are entitled to their opinions—if one of your respondents has a certain image of you, then a recruiter or interviewer might easily do so too, so accept the feedback with good grace—even if you need to grit your teeth and pretend to smile to do so. And always finish by thanking them for their honesty.

CONSIDER THE BIGGER PICTURE

Job-hunting is like trying to shoot a target with a gun. That gun could be a shotgun, scattering pellets in all directions with the vague hope of hitting something, anything. Or that gun could be a sniper's rifle, aimed at precisely the right target. Guess which approach I think you should be taking?

While the scattergun approach might work for entry-level positions, as a professional or a manager, you need to avoid wasting your energies by applying for every slightly relevant job you come across. If you want to build a career rather than merely get a new job, you need to think about exactly what you want.

Getting feedback is about establishing your strengths and weaknesses. But what do you like or dislike, want or need from your work? Putting your skills aside for a moment, what do you actually enjoy doing and want from your future in five, ten, or twenty years' time?

I coach many individuals who find themselves trapped into applying for jobs that are merely the predictable continuation of what they have been doing in the past. Ten years' experience as a sales manager? Then apply to be a sales director somewhere. Sixteen years as director of supply chain and logistics? Then apply to be a director in a bigger company.

But a growing number of professionals are beginning to question whether the future necessitates more of the same. I know a management consultant who is retraining as an acupuncturist, a market researcher who is moving into aid work, an ex-chemist who is now a top corporate lawyer. And then there are plenty of executives who are becoming freelancers or setting up their own businesses.

Let me ask you a question now. It's one of the standard interview questions and I'm sure you've been asked it before: "Where do you see yourself in five years' time?" And of course you know that the correct answer in an interview situation is to tell the interviewers what you think they want to hear. But let's ask you the same question for a different reason. Where do you really want to be in five years' time?

What are your life goals? What are your unfulfilled dreams and aspirations? Think about it. Reflect, consider, and imagine what your life and career could be like. Because it would be such a waste for you to reach the end of your career and wish that you could have done it all differently.

DECIDE ON YOUR PRIORITIES

Are you a hot lover, a bad parent, a born leader, or a freak of nature? Most people quite enjoy the kind of quizzes that you get in glossy magazines. I'm sure you know the sort—tick some boxes, add up your score, and discover your type. So here's my version—and it's designed to help you figure out what you might want from your next job.

In no particular order, here's a list of life priorities—some that you might find in a job and some that might conflict with your job. Tick, circle, or copy to a separate sheet of paper the ten that are most important to you:

- Autonomy—having freedom to act independently.
- Supportive colleagues—being in a team that respects and looks after you.
- Travel—being able to journey as part of your work.
- Equity—having ownership within a business.
- Family—your partner, children, and other significant relationships outside of work.
- Responsibility—being able to make decisions and influence strategy and direction.
- Location—having a geographic location that suits your needs.
- Camaraderie—having colleagues who are not only supportive at work, but also friends outside of it.

- Size of company—working for a small, medium, or international business.
- Leisure time—having evenings, weekends, and holidays to pursue personal interests.
- Power—having authority and control over your environment and others.
- Contribution to society—working on projects that have social worth.
- Order—having processes and procedures at work that allow you to be organized and efficient.
- Advancement—seeking promotion and upward mobility.
- Predictable work—having a routine or working pattern that agrees with you.
- Ethics—having work that embraces a set of values.
- Job security—having a position that offers long-term career stability.
- Leadership—managing others.
- Spiritual growth—developing spiritually and personally.
- Care—being able to show warmth, consideration, or nurturing for others.
- Money—receiving more financial reward for your efforts.
- Recognition—wanting to receive credit and appreciation for your work.
- Achievement—being able to complete goals or projects.
- Creativity—being able to apply your imagination and vision to concepts and ideas.

  - Variety—needing work that offers new challenges and activities.

Now take your shortlist of only ten items and rank them, rewriting them into a list from critically important to your life at the top to least important (but still more important than the others that you have discarded) at the bottom. People sometimes ask me whether they can have tied rankings, but I always say no. Life is tough. There are only 24 hours in the day and you can't have it all. Want to make your millions? Well, you better be prepared to give up those leisurely evenings and weekends. Want to be a great parent? Well, stop working those crazy hours in the office.

Of course your list of priorities probably doesn't tell you anything that you didn't already suspect. But keep it in mind and close to hand when you think about the kinds of roles and organizations that you apply for.

HONE YOUR VISION

What do you want to do before you die? Organizations talk about having visions, missions, and values. But in day-to-day life, people are more likely to talk about having aspirations, dreams, or perhaps "stuff that they want to do before they die."

Justin, a management consultant, decided to write his own eulogy as an exercise in figuring how he wanted to be remembered by the time he died. On reflection, he found that he didn't want to be remembered for helping businesses increase their market share and profits. He's now retraining as a psychodynamic counselor.

So try to encapsulate what you want from your next job by creating a vision. I know it sounds cheesy, but no one else ever needs to know about it. Neither do you have to write it as a piece of prose; a list of meaningful bullet points can work just as well. But do make sure that your vision is phrased positively—about what you do want to do—rather than about what you don't want to do or need to avoid. If you take the time to work through your vision, I guarantee that it will help you to keep your job hunt on track.

Your vision should try to capture as many elements about your next job as you can. It will certainly take into account the ranked priorities from the previous exercise as well as the industry sectors and types of culture you would wish to work in. But it should also consider why you want this next job. For example, is it a stepping stone to the job after? Or is it a job that will allow you to wind down and spend more time to pursue life goals that have nothing to do with work?

Job-hunting isn't rocket science—this book can't fail to help you to find a job. But by writing a vision, you will help yourself to find the *right* job.

HAVE A PLAN

Imagine that you are one of the marketing team at a world-class company such as Procter & Gamble or Unilever. You have a vision, an idea of who your customers are. You have a product too. What next? Well, can you imagine them launching a new product without a carefully worked-through business plan? No. So neither should you try to launch yourself on the job market without one.

As you read the remaining chapters of this book, try to piece together a plan in your mind. Even better, write it out.

It doesn't need to be complicated. Break up your working week and think about how much time you can set aside for the job-hunting process. In those hours, what can you realistically achieve? When are you going to send your CV to particular agencies or pick up the telephone to re-ignite old contacts?

Management training courses always bleat on about setting SMART (specific, measurable, achievable, realistic, and timed) goals. And it's probably not a bad idea to keep in mind some of those tenets. What specifically will you do? How will you be able to measure whether your actions are paying off or not? What are some achievable and realistic goals for the different phases of your job search? And when will you tackle each element of the job search—from gathering feedback and delineating your vision to rewriting your CV, calling headhunters or contacting your network?

Put pen to paper and capture the major elements of your self-marketing plan. Vague intentions or a notional plan of action in your head are all very well. But a written plan often has more power to galvanize and mobilize you into action or at least make you feel guilty enough to get a move on. So what's stopping you from doing it?

CREATING A
WINNING CV

Continuing with the job search as marketing analogy, you need to think about your sales literature. Customers don't buy a product solely because the brochure says it is good—although a good brochure might encourage them to take a trip to a showroom or store.

Unfortunately, too many professionals pay scant attention to the singularly important piece of sales literature otherwise known as the curriculum vitae. It may be the case that no one ever got the job because of a great CV. But a bad or even average CV can quite easily rule you out of the equation.

Most of the job-hunters with whom I work have an outdated idea of what should go on a CV and merely add to it or amend it slightly every time they need to update it. The result is too often a mishmash of paragraphs and phrases that may no longer have any relevance to their current job search.

I'm not going to take you through every single step of writing a CV. I'm sure you know about basic guidelines such as the need to pack your CV with action words such as "analyzed" and "communicated," "developed" and "negotiated."

However, many of the more subtle rules of CV writing have changed. So discard everything you thought you knew about writing a CV and take note.

TAILOR YOUR CV

If you tend to create a single CV and submit it with different covering letters or emails to different jobs, then you are already going wrong. A CV should never be a completed document—it should always be a shifting, chameleon-like work in progress. The CV that you send to one organization might have little in common with the CV that you send to the next.

The *key* rule of writing a good CV is to ensure that it tells the reader exactly how you match up to their particular brief. In some circumstances, recruiters and headhunters may spend as little as a minute glancing at your CV. So make sure that your CV mentions all of the key phrases that the recruiters use in their job advert.

If a job advert asks for "leadership skills," then damn well make sure that you use that precise phrase a couple of times in the top half of the first page of your CV. Don't think that it is implicit that you have leadership skills simply because you say that you have "20 years of management experience." If another job talks about "communicating complex information," then use that exact same phrase rather than "good communication skills" – again somewhere in the top half of the first page of your CV.

You might think that a recruiter would be able to read between the lines. But CVs are often sifted by inexperienced recruitment minions or administrative staff who lack the experience to judge the difference between a good or bad candidate. So they may have been specifically instructed to look for certain key words and phrases—and to bin CVs that do not contain them.

To make it even easier for them, use different typefaces, font sizes, bold and underlining selectively to make those key phrases jump off the page. I cannot emphasize this point enough. Relying on a single CV across different roles and organizations will lower your response rate considerably. So it's up to you—can you be bothered to spend a few minutes tailoring your CV and inserting key words and phrases?

UNDERSTAND THAT SIZE MATTERS

In CVs, as in life, size matters. In the case of a CV though, small is beautiful; less is more. Having a lengthy CV packed with too much information serves only to distract recruiters and headhunters from locating what they need to know.

"If your CV is too long and verbose—more than five pages—then I assume you are verbose," says Suzzane Wood, a partner at executive search firm Heidrick & Struggles. "If it is too short and bullet pointed, then I think it reflects on your personality too."

A senior executive with 30 years' experience can get away with a four-page CV. More junior candidates should aim to produce no more than two or three pages.

And make sure that the finished product has plenty of white space on it. If the finished product doesn't have at least as much white space as the average fashion layout in the typical Sunday supplement, then you probably have too much information on it. Remember that a CV is supposed to whet the appetite of the reader, not force-feed them with information until they want to vomit.

One job-hunter, a 41-year-old director of marketing, had significantly reduced the widths of his margins, header and footer to pack more onto his CV. For someone who was so fastidious about the layout of his organization's website and brochures, I thought it ironic that he had failed to apply the same rules to this most personal item of sales literature. Just about the only way he could have squeezed more onto his CV would have been reducing the size of the font.

All of these tactics simply smack of desperation and an inability to pare your CV down to what is essential. So now you know.

START FROM SCRATCH

I was recently helping a client to shortlist candidates for a senior management job in the insurance industry. Amazingly, one of the candidates, a Vice President with responsibility for nearly 200 staff across nine branches, wasted as much space telling us about his experience in the period 1973 to 1979 as he did describing his current role. Now, he had already mentioned on the top of his CV that he had over 30 years' experience in the industry. So why waste space telling us about those very early days when he was just an office junior?

Another candidate, applying for a job of Director of Marketing Communications in a FTSE250 business, mentioned as one of his achievements that he "organized a trip to an international treasury management conference in Berlin"—back in 1985. Yes, it may have been relevant to other job applications at the tail end of the 1980s, but in the 21st century, the comment only served to generate a chuckle in the recruiting office.

Both of these candidates were applying for jobs with salaries well above the £60,000 mark. They were not stupid people. Neither were they unrepresentative of most of the CVs that I see.

I am constantly astounded by the amount of rubbish that candidates allow themselves to have on their CVs. And the reason is that most candidates amend and add to an existing CV rather than starting from scratch.

Think about what a recruiter wants to read on a CV. Do you really think that they need to know about your career history nearly two decades ago? Or that you passed A Levels in History, Economics and English? Even if you were applying for a job as a historian or economist, a recruiter won't want to know about your A Levels because they will be much more interested in your work experience.

There are many, many managers and professionals who believe that it is standard practice to include all of your work history, your exam results, and the like on a CV. But, unlike the North American résumé, there really is no single, standard format for a CV. There might have been a single format 20 years ago—but certainly not in today's job market.

Many job-hunters with whom I work argue that leaving information on a CV can't be harmful. And it probably won't harm your chances of getting a job in the sense of reducing your worthiness as a candidate. However, if a recruiter only has a minute to peruse your CV, then there is an opportunity cost to having unnecessary information on it. If they spend ten seconds reading (and possibly laughing at) some less relevant piece of information, that's ten seconds less to notice some directly important and hugely relevant item of information.

And that is why you should start a new CV from scratch. Tear off a blank sheet of paper and try to construct a CV to meet the needs of recruiters. Be ruthless with every piece of information on your CV. If it is not directly relevant to a particular vacancy, then leave it off.

KISS YOUR CV

If you have ever done any interviewing, you will know that CVs come in all shapes and sizes. From pink letter paper to having photos stapled to the top corner, perfumed paper, colored inks, and cartoons, I have (occasionally) seen them all.

However, the acronym KISS (keep it simple, stupid) serves us well when it comes to CV writing. Use standard A4 white paper. And pick a standard typeface such as Times (Times New Roman on a PC and Times Roman on a Mac), Palatino, or Helvetica (Arial on a PC).

Remember too that your CV should have plenty of white space, vaguely evoking the style and sensibilities of a glossy magazine layout. Use a small number of headings and occasional sub-headings. Allow yourself to use bold, capitalization, italics, and underlining only infrequently to draw attention to the half-dozen key words or phrases that you want recruiters to notice.

Now you may be able to cite examples of friends of friends that have allegedly used some clever gimmick with their CV to great effect. But outside of the creative industries, these are probably urban myths in a similar vein to the one about the friend of your cousin's husband's secretary's brother who went on holiday, got bitten by something, and ended up having a boil lanced to find that it was filled with hundreds of baby spiders. The truth is that 99.9 percent of candidates let the words on the page speak for themselves.

It's a question of substance over style. Do you want the substance of your CV to speak or the style to overwhelm the substance?

WEIGH UP DIFFERENT FORMATS

Patricia, a food service manager, was getting nowhere trying to apply for jobs in retail banking. Her experience was completely wrong for a career in the world of finance. But then she rewrote her CV completely—creating a section on "Achievements" that highlighted how she had met sales targets, coached and developed people, and improved customer satisfaction ratings. She buried the fact that she had done all of these in food service rather than banking until the very end of her new CV. And it worked in getting her interviews.

It is standard practice to write your name, address and contact details at the top of a CV. But, after that, the rest is up for grabs.

Most candidates tend to list their employment and education next in a reverse chronological format— mainly because that's just how it's always been done. But the past decade has seen the rise of a functional format that presents readers with a breakdown of your skills or competencies.

Before we do away with the reverse chronological format, let's consider some of its strengths and weaknesses. One of its strengths is that it is so popular—even novice interviewers feel comfortable gleaning information from one. And the format also confirms the continuity of your experience —for example, that you have had eight, ten or twenty years' unbroken experience in a certain field or profession.

But the reverse chronological format doesn't suit everyone. For a start, if you are trying to change profession, enter a new field or move into a different industry sector, recruiters will be able to tell immediately "you don't have the right experience." And it certainly exposes periods of unemployment or if you didn't stay long in any of your roles. Perhaps worst of all, it can imply that you have failed to progress and allowed your career to stagnate if you have been in one position for too long.

For these reasons, an alternative functional format can better suit some candidates. Begin by picking up the key—perhaps between three to six— skills you think your target employers are looking for. And then list them in a section entitled "Key skills" or "Competencies." If a job advert lists "coaching and development skills" as a prerequisite for the job then, lo and behold, you use those precise words as one of your skill headings.

You still need to list your employment history toward the end of your CV—taking up no more than a handful of lines, listing simply the names of your employers and dates. But the beauty of a functional format is that you can direct a reader's attention to your transferable skills rather than your lack of experience or any other issues.

So if you are trying to change the direction of your career, or perhaps took time out to raise a family, suffered a period of illness, or were demoted after a restructuring in your organization, the functional format might help to boost your chances of being invited to interviews.

Anyway, you are a bright person. So I shall let you decide on the essential format of your CV.

DEVISE YOUR OWN FORMAT

There really are no set rules about the content and ordering of a CV. If there are any rules, they are the rules of marketing—i.e. that it should draw attention to the strengths of the product and gloss over its weaknesses.

Advertisers do it all the time. After all, when was the last time you saw an advert for a car that admitted that you'd want to tear your hair out over the insurance premiums? Or an advert for a skincare product that acknowledges that it only makes you look younger and that it doesn't actually make you younger?

If the two most common CV formats—the reverse chronological and the functional—do not fit your needs, then don't use them. You can devise your own format to highlight your key achievements and either bury or gloss over embarrassing details.

A candidate with a perfectly "normal" career history might use the headings:

Name
Contact details
Employment history
Education
Other information

However, a (perhaps young) candidate with top-class exam results but little paid employment might choose to direct the reader's attention first to their education. And the label "work experience" could be used to highlight skills accumulated during unpaid work:

Name
Contact details
Education
Work experience
Interests

Another candidate might use the heading "accomplishments" to get across certain quantifiable career achievements in lieu of directly relevant experience. And the term "qualifications" might be appropriate for candidates who, perhaps having left school without passing many exams, have since accumulated relevant professional qualifications.

> Name
> Contact details
> Accomplishments
> Previous experience
> Qualifications

You probably get the picture by now. Don't just think of reordering the major sections of your CV and using different labels as additional options or "nice to haves" for enhancing the impact of your CV. Think of them as necessary and vital steps for enhancing your chances of getting invited to interviews.

QUANTIFY YOUR ACHIEVEMENTS

"Experience is less important than what you've achieved," says Ashley Summerfield at executive search firm Egon Zehnder International. "A CV that says 'seven years in sales and marketing' only tells me that you didn't get fired in that time. What did you achieve in that time?"

Employers use all sorts of language to talk about what they want from their workforces. They talk about ideas such as diversity, teamwork, and innovation. But at the end of the day, they all really want the same thing. They want to employ people who can help them to achieve their goals. They want to pick candidates who have a track record of delivering results.

Think about all of the achievements and accomplishments that you have produced at work. But remember that it's not an achievement to have devised some new process or procedure, system or scheme. It's only an achievement if doing so helped the organization achieve its stated goals.

For most businesses, their goals are fairly transparent—they're usually about increasing profits or shareholder return. And you can demonstrate that you can contribute to those goals by having increased revenues or sales. Or perhaps by having slashed overheads and reduced costs too. Increased efficiency and enhanced productivity are worth mentioning too.

The most impressive achievements always relate to the bottom line. But if you can't demonstrate an impact on the bottom line, then think about accomplishments such as having created new products, improving workplace safety, growing market share, improving customer satisfaction or retention, reducing employee turnover, or raising a team's morale.

And make sure that you quantify your achievement by attaching figures to it. Was it a 2.4 percent improvement in net margin or a 12 percent reduction in employee turnover? A 38 percent increase in customer retention or a 1.3 percent increase in market share?

Make sure that your CV communicates in no uncertain terms the benefits that you would bring to an employer. Don't just talk vaguely about the skills that you possess. Talk about how you have used your skills to achieve measurable results.

SUMMARIZE YOUR EXPERIENCE

Just as a song on the radio often has a catchy chorus or a newspaper article has a headline, your CV needs a hook to snare the interest of the recruiter picking up your CV. And that's the role of a profile or summary statement.

A fairly recent development, a profile should try to capture within no more than three or four sentences exactly why you are perfect for a particular job. The written equivalent of a face-to-face elevator speech, it's your chance to pitch yourself to a recruiter in just ten seconds. A good profile alerts a recruiter to pay more attention, to slow down and give your CV a few more seconds of their precious time. A poorly written or irrelevant profile encourages them to add your CV to their reject pile almost straightaway.

The last time I applied for a job was quite a few years ago. But here is my verbatim profile from the last time I put together a CV: "I am a chartered psychologist with considerable experience of assessing and developing blue chip clients. I previously worked as a consultant at The Boston Consulting Group."

I was trying to get across a number of key facts to my target employers. Firstly that I was chartered and had "considerable"—as opposed to just a handful of years'—experience of consulting. Secondly, I mentioned "assessing" and "developing," which are two particular areas of expertise within the field of business psychology. "Blue chip clients" is an attempt to reassure employers that I worked with big and impressive clients as opposed to pokey local concerns. And mentioning "The Boston Consulting Group" is my attempt to get them to delve further into my CV, because the other consultancies that I worked for were not businesses that employers would necessarily recognize.

Here's another example, this time written in the third person: "A general manager with more than 20 years' experience of delivering targets in the distribution sector. Currently responsible for revenues of over £108 million and coaching and developing 165 staff. Exceeded financial targets in four out of the last five years."

I'm sure that you get the idea by now. Your profile needs to demonstrate how you fulfill the recruiter's every need. Just remember to amend and tailor your profile to meet the needs of each and every employer.

SELECT INTERESTS AND HOBBIES WITH CARE

Do you think that a recruiter wants to know (and these are all real examples) that you "relax by playing the guitar and writing songs", or that you "enjoy watching most sport"? How about the fact that you used to be "university tennis captain" (over 20 years ago) or that you try to "spend as much time with my family as my job permits"?

All of these examples come from the CVs of managers, professionals, and executives. None of them earned less than £60,000 a year when their CVs came across my desk.

Most people feel compelled to include some of their hobbies and interests in an attempt to show that they are rounded people. You could argue that none of these on a CV are strictly damaging to your chances. But do you honestly believe that irrelevant interests will boost your chances of being invited to an interview? Can you imagine a pair of recruiters in a room nodding and agreeing that playing a musical instrument or a demonstrable commitment to their family makes them a stronger candidate for the job? No. Of course not. And so such information only serves to draw attention away from the more important details on your CV. Bearing in mind that there is an opportunity cost to including less relevant information, I would strongly urge you to delete unnecessary interests or hobbies.

The exceptions to the rule are sporting accolades that are relatively fresh on your CV—especially if you achieved them in team sports. A lot of recruiters believe that team sports are proof positive of teamworking ability in the workplace. But if it's more than ten years in the past, then including it just makes you seem old and sad.

Relevant interests should also be highlighted. For example, a candidate for a high-profile job in insurance mentioned that he was "a member of the Insurance Golf Club of Glasgow." Hmm. Yes, I suppose it could be taken as evidence of his networking ability. But unfortunately he had just listed the achievement, rather than explaining that it was evidence of his networking ability.

A line manager within the industry might immediately understand the relevance of being a member of the insurance golf club. But keep in mind that CVs are usually sifted by human resources administrators or external consultants who may not understand the precise ins and outs of your particular industry. Consequently, for the achievements that you do include, make sure that it is blatantly obvious to non-specialist readers what they mean or why they might be important.

PONDER ON YOUR MARITAL STATUS

I know of a number of line managers who have rather strange beliefs on the topic of candidates' marital status. Now this is an area that most organizations would vehemently deny ever influences their decision-making. But you and I both know that what an organization espouses and what its managers actually do are often two very separate issues.

If you are a man and over 30 years of age, being married might be taken as a sign of stability and maturity—a plus point for management positions. However, if you are a man, under 30 and married, it could be taken as evidence that you have fallen into a relationship too young and are therefore prone to taking risky decisions.

Unfortunately, in job-hunting as in the world of work, women suffer worse than men when it comes to mentioning marital status. Line managers often worry that a married woman approaching the age of 30 may soon want to have children—with all the costs of maternity pay and recruiting a temporary replacement. It's illegal for them to ask you—either in a written application or in person during an interview—whether you plan to have children. But they might make that assumption anyway and nudge you off their shortlist.

And if you are a woman over 35 and single, I have heard more than one manager (often in macho environments such as investment banking or management consulting) make comments about the candidate obviously being unattractive and unable to land a husband.

Of course all of these perceptions are deeply unfair. But please don't shoot the messenger—I only relay what I hear.

It is not a legal requirement to mention your marital status. Neither do you need to mention the number of children that you have or their ages. Many candidates include this information only because it used to be traditional to do so. But unless you are a married man aged over 30, you might do better to avoid disclosing your marital status.

BE SENSIBLE AND SAFE

I have seen genuine email addresses on CVs for management jobs that have included "kyliesfanclub" and "doctor_spanky." The names of the internet service providers aren't important (and if I mentioned them then you might be tempted to email these poor people). But I'm sure you get the picture.

While your email moniker may seem like a feat of cunning linguistics that showcases your irony or ability to pun, it could fall far short of impressing recruiters. Especially in customer-facing businesses, I know of more than one human resources director who sees them as a failure on the part of applicants to think about their first impact on others. Long before you get to meet someone face to face and electrify them with your quirky sense of humor, you might already have created the impression that you are a bit of a loose cannon.

And joke email addresses are dangerous for another, more practical, reason too. The organization's anti-spam email could filter your email address out; your application might get re-routed into a spam folder and of course you would have no way of knowing.

Enough said.

LIE AT YOUR OWN RISK

Telling lies on your CV can be risky business.

"We always do education checks for shortlisted candidates and when people haven't been honest it causes traffic accidents," warns Luke Meynell, partner and head of the UK board practice at Russell Reynolds Associates. "For example, we had a candidate who changed a 2:2 into a 2:1 because he felt he would be precluded otherwise, which he wouldn't have been. But when we found out, he had to withdraw."

On the other hand, not everyone gets caught. I know a job-hunter who left university with a third-class degree in physics. Despite this, he managed to get a job first as an internal consultant for a major retail bank and is now close to achieving partnership within the consulting division of one of the Big Four accountancy firms. And he achieved it simply by lying about his degree class.

For senior or high-profile roles, an organization will undoubtedly check your education and run multiple reference checks. At Russell Reynolds Associates, for example, as well as a standard education check, they often ask up to ten references to comment on the performance of a single candidate.

Many large organizations ask to see examination certificates as a matter of course. But, then again, many organizations don't and a surprising number of people do manage to get away with lies ranging from slight exaggerations to blatant untruths.

Lying is obviously morally reprehensible. But then again, a lot of what goes on in business isn't always above board. In reality, whether you decide to massage the truth on your CV comes down to a judgment call. Just make sure you think it through first.

OMIT UNNECESSARY INFORMATION

"Age doesn't matter unless you're a cheese," said some actress by the name of Billie Burke. I have to admit that I don't recall any of her work, but the saying made me laugh. Unfortunately, clever little aphorisms count for nothing in the harsh world of real business. Employers do have ideal ages in their heads. And if you stick your age at the top of your CV, you might be doing yourself a disservice.

Of course it is illegal to discriminate on the basis of age. But how would you know if that had happened?

So why bother mentioning your age at all? New legislation that came into law in 2006 means that recruiters are no longer allowed to ask for your age. And if you are too old or too young for what the recruiter has in mind, they could use it to discriminate against you. So put your work history and achievements at the top of the CV—let your experience speak to them first. And if they really want to work out your age, they can usually do it by working backwards from the dates of your education or length of employment. So don't waste space telling them how old you are. Give your CV more white space instead.

Be ruthless with every phrase on your CV. Keep in mind the opportunity cost of having it on your CV. If a single word isn't directly relevant, get rid of it to prevent it distracting a recruiter from spotting the key information that they are looking for.

Unless you are a graduate with no work experience, then don't include details of your referees. Heck, don't even bother stating "references available on request" as that is assumed by most recruiters.

The same goes for your age.

Don't even think about mentioning internal courses that you attended. Saying that you attended a course only indicates that you were physically present. It doesn't mean that you learned anything or can put those skills to good use. Courses are features of your career, not benefits to potential employers. So what benefits could you describe on your CV instead?

Show no mercy as you go through every single line of your CV.

GET A SECOND OPINION

Nearly finished. But what if I said to you that you might just need to do it all again?

Having invested time and energy in your CV, you are probably quite proud of it. But remember that pride comes before a fall. You may be too close to your CV to have any objectivity about how good it is in absolute terms. And you don't want to have to be turned down by a handful of employers before realizing that not all is right with your CV.

Just as it's a good idea to get feedback on the personal strengths and weaknesses of you as a product, try to get some feedback on your CV too. But don't approach friends and family as they are unlikely to be able to offer you the level of objectivity that you need. They know you too well and may hesitate to criticize the fruit of your labors.

A better idea is to ask your friends to pass your CV on to contacts of theirs who do not know you at all and who are involved in interviewing candidates at your level. Email your friends a copy of your CV along with a brief description of the kind of position that you are looking for, as well as a rough idea of the salary band.

Your friends' contacts should then relay back to your friends the kind of person whom they see coming through from your CV. What do they see as your strengths and shortcomings? What doubts or queries does the CV raise in their minds? To what extent do they see a good fit between the person whom your CV tries to portray and the kind of position that you are looking for?

Ask your friends to gather as much feedback as possible. Tell them that "it looks great" isn't good enough feedback. Encourage them to probe deeper and to push for more negatives than positives. After all, you could get positives from your mother. It's the negatives that will help to fine-tune your CV.

This is a time-consuming exercise, and begs favors from a number of your friends. And remember that it is critical to ask your friends to seek contacts who are involved in interviewing at your level rather than just friends of theirs. But trust me— this exercise will help to strip away wordiness and irrelevance from your CV and increase your chances of landing interviews.

EXPLAIN YOUR EMPLOYABILITY

A great CV should make a recruiter sit up like you had thrown a glass of water in their face. However, letters still play an important role in fleshing out precisely why you are right for any particular vacancy.

Oddly enough, I would say that the average graduate writes clearer and more interesting letters than the average manager or experienced professional. In retrospect, it makes sense. Current graduates are schooled by their careers services on how to write letters designed to maximize their chances. Most seasoned office workers are more used to using bullet points, preparing reports and presentations, and writing letters designed to inform than to whet the appetite and pique the interest of the reader.

Your basic covering letter should consist of no more than four or five short paragraphs on a single sheet of paper. For those of you who wish to have the briefest of reminders, here's an example covering letter:

Dear Mr Smith,

1. **General Manager, ABC Company**

2. I read with great interest your recent advert in the *Sunday Times*. Given my experience in having turned around a similar-sized retail business here at XYZ Company, I believe that I am a strong candidate for this position.

3. Three years ago, I took on a business unit that was failing to achieve both its revenue and profit targets. Since then, I have turned it around and it is now one of the strongest performing business units in the group. Last year we exceeded our profit targets by over 5 percent. In doing so, we also boosted customer satisfaction with our services to over 95 percent—again exceeding our targets by more than 6 percent.

4. As you will be able to see from my CV, I have extensive experience of new product development—from the inception of new ideas through to market testing and subsequent launch. In addition, I take great pride in my ability to have revitalized management teams and boosted team morale.

5. I would very much like the opportunity to meet with you in person and tell you

more about what I believe I can contribute to the business. If you have any more questions, please don't hesitate to get in touch with me. I appreciate your time in reading this and I look forward to hearing from you soon.

6. Yours sincerely,

Pat Jones

Points as follows:

1. Refer to the position for which you are applying. Highlight this in bold so that your letter and CV find their way to the right recruiter.
2. Demonstrate how you know about the position and the company in no more than a few sentences. The very best opening paragraph would mention that you came across the opportunity because someone who knows both you and the recipient of the letter suggested that the two of you should get together. But I shall discuss this in more detail in the next part of this book, Opening Up Opportunities.
3. Highlight and expand on the two areas of your CV that you believe state best why the recruiter should invite you to an interview. You might want to highlight the length of your experience, skills, or particularly

pertinent technical expertise, or perhaps past achievements that would be of direct benefit to this specific employer.

4. Go on to mention a further one or two reasons to back up your argument. However, remember that your big guns should be employed in the earlier paragraph.

5. Express your keen interest in the position and make yourself as available as possible.

6. Just the briefest of reminders that if you are naming the recipient of a letter, always finish off with "Yours sincerely." "Yours faithfully" is appropriate only if you are writing "Dear Sir/Madam" at the top of the letter.

Don't underestimate either the importance or burden of writing a good covering letter.

AIM FOR ONE IN FOUR

As a switched-on professional, you're probably used to exceeding goals. So here's one more for you. With proper tailoring of your CV, you should get invited to at least one out of every four jobs that you apply for. To some readers, that may sound low—but remember that the rule of thumb is to aim for at least one in four. Of course, four out of four is the ultimate goal here.

To other readers, that may sound like a high number, given that most jobs receive dozens if not hundreds of applications. But assuming that you aren't targeting completely the wrong industry or trying to leap too many rungs on the corporate ladder in one go, I would say that one in four is totally achievable for managerial and professional job-hunters.

Bear in mind that many jobs will receive CVs cobbled together from parts of older CVs that could be a couple of decades out of date. And because these people have grown accustomed to those words and phrases, they fail to see that most of the information is hopelessly irrelevant. Or perhaps they are simply too lazy to tailor each and every one of their CVs to meet the needs of different employers.

One in four. Make no excuses. Now just go and do it.

OPENING UP
OPPORTUNITIES

In job-hunting, as in life, there is news both good and bad. The good news is that the job market provides a world of opportunities for talented individuals. But the bad news is that it takes serious work to find those opportunities, as most of these lie within the huge "hidden market" of jobs that are never advertised. A lot of employers find that the payback simply isn't good enough for advertising in the press or online. Instead, employers often pay headhunters and agencies or rely on speculative applications, word of mouth, and approaching people they already know.

"For us as an employer, our preference is to find candidates through referrals or recommendations rather than agencies or other means," says Carol-Ann White, Global HR Director at public relations business LEWIS. "So networking through contacts and going to events is key to getting a job."

Some estimates claim that the hidden market could account for up to 80 percent of all jobs. Now, we all know that there are lies, damned lies, and statistics. But whatever the precise figure, you can be certain that it is a significant proportion of jobs that are filled by word of mouth.

And even when jobs are advertised, you may have less of a chance than you think. I know of more than one organization that has placed an advert knowing full well that they will ultimately fill the vacancy with someone who is already known to them. The advert and subsequent interviewing process are often designed solely to satisfy internal stakeholders (often within human resources) who believe in equal opportunities and doing what is "fair" or "right."

The proportion of jobs that are never advertised seems to grow in proportion to the seniority of positions too. Graduate jobs within large organizations are hardly ever filled by word of mouth; however, senior managers are more likely to listen to the recommendation of someone whom they know and trust. In addition, senior managers often keep an eye on talented individuals within competitor organizations in case they should ever need to replace key people within their own organizations.

"Self promotion is not rocket science, but it works," advises Sue Shipley, a partner at executive search firm Odgers, Ray & Berndtson. "The best people are very preemptive in their careers. They know what they want and develop a plan for getting other people to hear about what they have done."

Many job-hunters immediately counter that they don't know anyone "important." Or that they didn't attend a posh school or belong to an exclusive club. But the whole point of networking is that you don't need to have important contacts. Just because you don't know anyone "important" doesn't mean that you might not know someone who knows someone who knows someone who is "important." Networking is merely about using those links between people to broaden your job search.

It's time-consuming and it is hard work. But networking is also ultimately one of the most valuable tools at your disposal for tracking down a great job.

JFDI

"Active networking is a key channel for finding a new job. Of course face-to-face meetings are more powerful than just sending in your CV. But candidates feel it's inappropriate to hawk themselves around the job market," says Luke Meynell at Russell Reynolds Associates. "They feel reluctant to market themselves in the same way that they would market their product or business, but they have a duty to market themselves in the best way possible."

Georgina, an IT training executive, admits: "I hate feeling that I need to ask for help. However, when people ask me for help I'm always delighted to help them. So it's probably a psychological barrier that I need to overcome."

Many managers and executives feel uncomfortable with the idea of networking, saying that they feel unaccustomed to asking for help. Others want to keep it secret from their friends and contacts that they may be unhappy in their job or out of work. A few feel that it borders on begging or is in some way beneath them. But the fact is that networking delivers results. All of these are hang-ups with you, not the people whom you will be speaking to. And while some networkers do come across as desperate and needy (and therefore never get anywhere with their attempts to network), effective networkers know never to ask for a job, but instead to ask for information.

Networking is simply about approaching people and making use of personal recommendations.

And if you invest the time and effort in doing it properly, you will find that dozens of your friends and ex-colleagues, contacts and acquaintances will be more than happy to keep their eyes and ears open for opportunities on your behalf.

Networking may be hard work in the sense of having to summon up the courage to approach people. But it's not hard in one sense: you do not need to acquire dramatically new skills as if you were learning to perform open-heart surgery or walk a tightrope. You already possess all of the skills you need to network. It just takes a bit of drive and determination on your part to make it happen.

And what's the worst that could happen? Sure, someone might refuse to help you. But so long as you follow some basic principles and remain relentlessly courteous, your contacts are unlikely to take offense.

And the best that could happen? Someone could point your way in the direction of your dream job.

So, to borrow from the strapline of the world's largest branded sportswear company (but, at the same time, apologizing profusely to their legal team), "just f***ing do it."

CONSIDER THE DIFFERENT AREAS OF YOUR LIFE

It's easy to get started networking: make a list of everyone you know. Yes, everyone. And write it down— don't try to hold your list in your head. It will take a while, but it will be worth the effort.

Think about the many different facets of your life. Of course your work contacts will form a large chunk of your networking list. But don't just limit your thinking to people in your current organization and previous employers. Think about ex-colleagues and customers past and present. And don't forget suppliers and other business acquaintances including accountants, bankers, and lawyers.

Outside of work, try to recall the people you know from school, college, and higher education. Then there are the people you know from sports clubs, unions, voluntary associations, community groups, or religious organizations. And of course there are your family, relatives, and even neighbors too.

Think of the listing exercise as a one-person brainstorming session. You probably know that true brainstorming sessions are supposed to encourage people to throw all ideas—no matter how bizarre or impractical they might at first seem—into the discussion in the hope of setting off further ideas. And the same goes for this initial stage of creating your networking list. Jotting down one supposedly unimportant name might just call to mind another name or remind you that they are married to someone or work with someone who might be very important.

The key here is to be as comprehensive as possible. Never exclude anyone from your list because you don't think they will be able to help.

DEVELOP YOUR SPIEL

Okay, so you call a contact. Ring, ring. Ring, ring. Click. They pick up and say "Hello?" Over to you. What are you going to say?

Networking differs from merely chatting to people because networking has a purpose. So what specifically will you say when your contact picks up the telephone?

Of course your ultimate objective is to find a job. But one of the quickest ways to make your contacts feel uncomfortable and reluctant to help you further is to ask them directly for a job. The vast majority of your contacts will not be recruiters. And even if they are, they are unlikely to be looking for people exactly like you. So never ask directly for a job.

A better bet is to ask for information. Think about what specific knowledge would help you to further your job search. You might want to find out about trends and developments in your target sector. Perhaps you would like advice on how to improve the wording of your CV and covering letters in approaching a particular organization. Maybe you want the name and contact details of the right manager to approach or an introduction to that individual. On occasion it might even be appropriate to talk about salaries—tell contacts that you are trying to benchmark salaries in your field or sector.

Whatever you are looking for, make sure that you have a word-perfect spiel to introduce yourself and get your message across.

Try to think through the precise words and phrases that you will use to capture your contacts' attention and solicit their help. Many people find it helps to write a spiel out in prose form and read it out loud to ensure that it is clear and succinct.

So, let's give it a go. Who are you and why are you calling?

PRIORITIZE YOUR LIST

Not all of your contacts are created equal. Your close friend who happens to be the human resources director of a competitor company might be a better first port of call than a distant friend from university who has since decided to live in a hippy commune.

When networking, it helps to be fairly ruthless in prioritizing whom you decide to get in touch with first.

Start by splitting your list into two parts, based on the strength of your relationship with them. The first part of your list should be people with whom you feel you have strong or at least good relationships. Perhaps they are close friends, recent colleagues, or at least business acquaintances with whom you have had some meaningful dealings.

Then go through the two parts of your list assigning a rating of perceived value to each name. You can use whatever rating system you feel comfortable with. But most job-hunters use a simple "A," "B," or "C" system to single out individuals who are very important, a little important, or not very important.

For example, the aforementioned human resources director would make it to the first part of your list because of your close relationship and an "A" rating because of the nature of their job. Using the same system, you may never need to get in touch with your distant-friend-cum-hippy.

START OFF GENTLY

A good way to start networking is to pick from your list the names of a dozen people whom you feel extremely comfortable approaching. If you are at all nervous about the prospect of networking or unfamiliar with the process, why make life difficult for yourself by trying to get in touch with the most important contacts on your list? Start with lower-priority close friends or perhaps even family members and ease yourself up that learning curve.

Okay, a family member may not work in your field and probably won't have industry-relevant information to pass on to you. But you can still ask them for referrals to people who might be able to help. The idea of starting with this receptive group of people is as much to familiarize yourself with your networking spiel as it is to gather critically useful information.

A lot of job hunters are tempted to go through all of their current and previous work contacts in an effort to avoid approaching their social or family contacts. But you already have a strong bond with your friends and family, so why wouldn't they want to help you out?

After your first dozen people, take a break to review your progress. What were you pleased with? What could you have said or done differently? Are you completely satisfied that you sounded natural and confident, intelligent and articulate?

There's compelling research to back up the fact that people are often less influenced by what you say than how you say it. Make sure that you inject appropriate levels of energy and enthusiasm into your voice. Networking is not just about gathering information; it is as much about transmitting your enthusiasm and employability. After all, if you received a call from a would-be networker, would you want to refer them on if they sounded unhappy, dejected, or needy?

Once you are completely comfortable with both what you are saying and how you are saying it, you can then start to tackle some of the "A"-rated contacts on your list.

INTRODUCE YOURSELF APPROPRIATELY

It happened to me just the other day. I got a call and someone said, "Hello Rob, it's Martin Smith here."

Er ... Who?

Your closest friends obviously know who you are. They might already know that you are looking for a job too. But without a bit of a brief description, your more distant friends and contacts might need a gentle reminder as to how they know you. An introduction is even more important if you plan to approach the contacts of your contacts.

So before you decide to pick up the telephone, consider whether you might need to send a brief email or perhaps a letter warning them that you are going to get in touch. There is nothing more embarrassing for your contacts than receiving a telephone call and not being able to remember who you are or how they know you. But never send your CV unless a contact specifically asks for it. Sending your CV without an invitation screams, "I need a job" and will close more doors than it will open.

Here's a sample email with a breakdown of the purpose of each paragraph:

Dear Sarah,

1. Your name was suggested to me by Jonathan Gunderson because he says that you seem to know everyone in the world of retail marketing.

2. My background has been in financial marketing, but I am particularly interested in finding out more about marketing in industries such as retail. Jonathan suggested that you might be able to share some of your thoughts with me.

3. It would help me greatly if you could spare about 15 minutes of your time to speak with me on the telephone. I want to assure you that I'm not asking you for a job—just information.

4. I will give you a call next week to book a slot in your diary that would suit you.

Yours sincerely,

Peter Johnson

Points as follows:

1. Gain credibility with a contact immediately by mentioning the name of someone that they will recognize. Mentioning a specific name also ensures that your letter will reach your contact as opposed to being filtered out by an overefficient secretary or assistant.
2. Explain who you are and a little about what you are looking for.
3. Reassure the contact that you are not going to ask for a job, which is often the single biggest worry of most contacts when they are asked for help in such situations.
4. Warn the contact that you will be getting in touch soon. And then make sure that you do follow up with your phone call.

PRESS THE FLESH

Hmmm. Press the flesh. Sounds rather unsavory perhaps. But humans are social creatures. So it shouldn't surprise you to hear that networking works best when you can meet contacts face to face. They are more likely to remember you if they can put a face to the name.

And it is only when you meet that you can really impress upon your contacts positive qualities such as your professionalism, intelligence, and commitment to the job. So in all of your interactions, try to push for more interaction. Email is a beguiling tool and it is easy to sit at your computer believing that you have initiated "contact" with lots of people, when the truth is that your emails will be given no more than a few seconds of thought before being deleted and forgotten.

If you are exchanging emails with a contact, suggest a telephone conversation. Assure them that you will take up no more than 20 minutes of their time. Or if you are already conversing by telephone, ask for a short meeting. Promise them that it will take no more than half an hour of their time. And offer to travel to their offices or to meet them for a coffee in the morning or a drink in the evening. But if they seem at all reluctant, then don't try to pressurize them; settle instead for what they are willing to give you.

But in trying to set up meetings or even telephone conversations, never underestimate the power of gatekeepers. Secretaries and personal assistants are paid to screen sales people and corporate beggars. Be unfailingly polite to them. Introduce yourself, ask for their name, and engage in a little chat or banter if it seems appropriate. Do your utmost to ensure that they are on your side when it comes to trying to fit you into their boss's busy schedule.

Of course, when it comes to meeting people in the flesh, be as active at conferences and shows, association and alumni meetings, committee and charitable events as possible too, never forgetting the key principle of networking. Even if some of the people whom you meet at an event are not "important," they may be able to refer you on to a contact who knows yet another contact who is very, very important.

OBSERVE THE ETIQUETTE OF NETWORKING

"I'd agreed as a favor to a mutual contact to meet a job-hunter," says Adam, head of strategic planning within a retail plc. "But I was quite taken aback at his lack of preparation. He sat there smiling at me, as if he expected me to hand over a job or walk him through how to get a job. It was quite astounding really."

Whether you are meeting a contact in person or speaking to them on the phone, make sure that you treat the interaction with as much professionalism and attention to detail as if it were an interview for a job. After all, these contacts have to be so impressed by meeting you that they would be willing to refer you to their contacts or recommend you for jobs.

"We prefer to see people through personal referral because headhunters cost us money. Networking and referrals are extremely important and you'd be amazed at how generous even senior people can be with their time," advises Nicola Forristal, HR Director at BBH. "But don't just plonk yourself in front of someone. Have a point of view and bring something to contribute to the meeting rather than acting as a drain from a senior person."

Write out a list of questions that you want to ask each particular contact before you call or meet with them. Try to script broad, open-ended questions that will make a contact want to talk and wax lyrical, rather than closed questions that invite simple "yes" or "no" responses. And think of follow-up questions to ensure that you can facilitate the discussion and encourage them to think laterally about ways that they could help you.

When you do speak or meet, check how much time your contact has for the discussion too. It may seem like a nicety to do so, but keep in mind that your contact is giving you their time for free.

Take notes during your conversation too. You will be having discussions with many people and you will find it almost impossible to keep track of people, places, and information without notes. Also, when you're meeting someone in person, note-taking shows very visibly that you are hanging on their every word and extracting value from the meeting.

But do also follow the lead of your contact as to the tone of the discussion. If your contact is business-like and seems rushed for time, then adopt a more formal tone of voice and manner and keep your discussion focused on the topic at hand. On the other hand, if a contact wants to engage in a little chat, then allow yourself to relax and be more conversational too. Building rapport can be as important as building a professional and credible impression.

However, the biggest unspoken rule of networking is to remain positive and enthusiastic. If you seem at all discouraged or downcast about your run of bad luck or the difficulty of the job-hunting process, your contact will inevitably be reluctant to introduce you to other contacts or recommend you for jobs. So be careful of revealing too much information or allowing your body language to show your true feelings.

ASK FOR REFERRALS

I know I keep banging on about it, but the principle of networking really is that you don't need to know anyone "important" to begin with. And so a key objective during any discussion is to try to get at least one or two new names from each contact.

But a contact's first response is almost certain to be that they don't know anyone who would be able to help. So you need to prompt them and offer up examples of contacts who have given you introductions or even just names that have led on to opportunities. And if a contact can't think of anyone within the course of your conversation, forestall a negative response by suggesting that your contact think about your request for a couple of days.

Referrals are important. So don't allow yourself to be fobbed off. Use all of your charm, cunning, and powers of persuasion to get some names.

And when they do come back with some names, ask if your contact would mind emailing or calling those new contacts to warn them that you will be getting in touch. And remember to end each discussion by thanking your contact sincerely for their time and effort in helping you out.

Networking works. There are plenty of job-hunters who testify to having made it work. However, if you find that many of your contacts are not willing to give you names of further contacts, then you need to consider what you are doing wrong. Networking is a tried and tested technique for obtaining information and accessing unadvertised jobs. So if it isn't working for you, I'm afraid the fault probably lies with you. Reflect on what might be going wrong. Are you explaining yourself clearly? Do you come across as at all needy or desperate? Are you expecting too much from your contacts and making them feel uncomfortable?

You could even get in touch with some of your earlier contacts and ask for some candid feedback on how you came across. Or try role-playing a networking conversation with a trusted business contact to see if you can identify what is going wrong. Whatever you do, don't simply give up on the notion of networking.

LINE UP YOUR REFERENCES

When you later get invited to interviews, potential employers may ultimately want to check your references. So now is a good time to start identifying people who may be able to speak on your behalf.

Your referees may fall into three broad categories.

- The first category comprises people who can confirm factual information about you— such as length of employment, absenteeism record, remuneration package, and the basic responsibilities of your job. Of course, it may not be appropriate to tell your current boss that you are looking for a new job. But you might be able to line up past bosses to substantiate basic facts about you.
- The second category consists of people who may be able to provide a personal character reference. These should still generally be work contacts, but should be willing to talk in more general terms about your reliability and other positive traits.
- The third and possibly most important category of referees covers people who can vouch for your credibility. They should be able to speak from first-hand experience of having seen you at work and be able to provide concrete examples that show off your skill at work.

As you work through your list of contacts, think about different people who can testify to different skills. Some of them may be colleagues. But clients or customers can often be more impressive. Suppliers might be appropriate too if your role involves a lot of dealings with them.

At this stage all you need do is ask contacts for permission to use them as referees. Bear in mind that this is a favor and no one is obliged to act as a referee. And remember to check that they would feel comfortable speaking about you in glowing terms. Don't just ask whether they will be a referee; ask whether they feel comfortable providing you with a positive reference. That way, you provide them with an escape route if they don't feel happy giving an unreservedly positive reference.

PREPARE YOUR REFEREES

You shouldn't be giving details of your referees out to employers until you are significantly progressed in discussions with them. Otherwise you could risk wearing out the good will of your referees with excessive calls from employers.

But once you have gained a contact's agreement to act as a referee, always send them an email with reminders of the facts or examples of what you might like them to talk about. Sending them a copy of your CV might not go amiss either.

For the first category of referees, make sure that both you and they are clear on key dates, your job title, responsibilities, and size of budget. It's worth checking these details in writing rather than over the telephone so that they can mull the information over and let you know if there are any areas of disagreement.

For the second and third categories of referees, give them a brief overview of the kinds of jobs you are looking for as well as the kinds of skills you would like them to emphasize when it comes time to speak with employers.

Don't forget to thank these contacts profusely for agreeing to provide references. And keep them warm with occasional updates on your job hunt to ensure that they remain primed and ready to speak on your behalf.

NEVER ASK FOR A JOB

Ever had a door slammed in your face? Ouch. I haven't, but I imagine that it hurts.

Of course we are talking about metaphorical doors. But one of the unspoken rules of networking is never to be too obvious in selling yourself to contacts. Never ask directly for a job. Doing so makes you sound needy and desperate. And it puts your contacts in a difficult position because the vast majority of them won't be able to help you with that particular request. Cue awkward silence etcetera.

Networking is a marketing tool that seeks to raise your profile in the minds of potential buyers. But it differs from product marketing in that networking is a much more subtle sell. Rather than directing a buyer's attention to your features and benefits, you can only hint at your skills and experience or discuss them if a contact asks you about them.

Your approach—whether by email or telephone—should always focus on the fact that you are looking for information and news about jobs rather than a job itself. The fact that your ultimate objective is actually to find a new job should always be implicit rather than rammed down the throats of your contacts.

You can politely ask a contact to let you know if they come across any contacts that might be looking to fill a vacancy. But only mention it once. If you have cause to get in touch with a contact for a second, third, or fourth time, don't mention it again. Your contacts are not stupid and reminding them that you are looking for a job will only make them feel uncomfortable. Remember that networking is about opening up opportunities in the "hidden market" and, as such, there are hidden rules that you need to obey.

BE READY TO BE INTERVIEWED

While you should never ask for a job, you should always be ready to be asked about your job. One of the joys of networking is that you never know when you may stumble upon a contact who does know of a job or indeed is in a position to offer a job.

If a contact asks you what you can bring to a sector, a company, or a role, how would you answer? Will you have a response that dazzles and impresses or one that starts "Er ... I hadn't really thought about it yet ..."?

Treat every networking conversation as a potential interview. If you are calling contacts, make sure to have a copy of your CV in front of you so you can refer to dates or details of your career history without hesitation. If you are meeting contacts in person, always dress in business-appropriate attire.

Don't be fazed if a contact suddenly starts to fire interview questions at you. Without realizing, you may just possibly have stumbled your way into an interview situation and the brink of a job offer.

REPEAT AS NECESSARY

If you make the effort to work your way through your list of contacts, you will exhaust your "A" list fairly quickly. But as a major goal of networking is to generate new contacts, you should never run out of more people to pursue. The process of networking relies on a multiplier effect—by asking each of your contacts for even a single contact, your network should easily double in size.

So in order to achieve your job-hunting goals, you just need to repeat as necessary.

But as your network grows and grows, you will need to establish a system to keep track of the many people you have spoken to and have yet to speak to. Many job-hunters use a spreadsheet or similar tool to capture information about their contacts—or at the very least about the "A"-rated ones. Cross-reference who has referred you to whom. Apart from their names and the date of your conversations, try to capture some information about their job, their history, background, and interests. How do your contacts know each other? And what's the nature of their relationship?

When you speak to the contacts of your contacts—effectively your contacts-once-removed—having a few nuggets of information about the person whom you both have in common could help to build just that little bit more rapport. Which could make all the difference between the new contact engaging in an in-depth and useful discussion as opposed to permitting you a brisk courtesy conversation.

Talking to these contacts-once-removed can be fairly nerve-wracking. Bear in mind that the two of you are pretty much strangers to each other. They don't know you and they certainly don't owe you anything. All you can offer in return for their time and insight is your gratitude, genuine interest in listening to what they have to say, and a little (subtle) flattery—perhaps about their clout in the industry or knowledge of the field.

MAINTAIN YOUR VISIBILITY

Someone once told me that polar bears hold one paw over their noses when they hunt. Their noses are black and the snow is white, so it might just be true that they don't want to alert their prey. On the other hand, someone might have been pulling my leg.

But unlike the polar bear, you want to maximize your visibility.

Networking can be a powerful tool for talking to new people. But it is not just about gathering information and gaining new contacts—it is also about turning existing contacts who merely know of you into advocates who would be willing to tell others about you and recommend you for jobs. And this is when you need to invest in some diligent slogging—in maintaining your visibility and reminding your many contacts that you exist.

A brief telephone conversation or a short meeting might keep you in the mind of a contact for a couple of days at most. A follow-up email might buy you an additional few moments in their short-term memory. So always follow up on your initial meeting or conversation by sending a short, handwritten thank-you letter. Don't even type the address on the envelope—there is something a little mysterious and evocative about an envelope with a handwritten address on it. Think about it for a moment—how many emails do you receive and delete with only a cursory glance every day? Compare that to the number of handwritten letters that you receive in a week or even a month. In an age of instantaneous and impersonal electronic missives, you will make yourself very much more memorable by putting pen to paper and sticking a stamp on an envelope.

But even a handwritten letter may only buy you a few more weeks of visibility. And this is where your note-taking comes into its own. If you make a note of each new contact's job and interests, background and concerns, you can use that information to maintain the relationship. In practice, most job-hunters simply don't have the time to do this for all of their contacts, but you should certainly try to do it for all of your "A"-rated contacts.

If you read a snippet of news about their company, why not drop them an email congratulating or commiserating with them? If you come across an article or a web link that your contact might be interested in, why not send it to them? Yes, you might argue that these are all slightly contrived methods of keeping in touch. But you're a smart person—work out the way to do it well!

SET AND ACHIEVE PERFORMANCE TARGETS

In your hunt for a new job, you will experience lows as well as highs. Many managers and professionals say that job-hunting is more daunting than their day-to-day jobs. Perhaps it is because it feels so much more personal when you are trying to market yourself rather than your organization's services or products. Or because job-hunting is so unpredictable and uncertain—it could be only a few weeks or many months before the right opportunity comes your way. And of course the pressure is that much greater if you find yourself having to leave one job before you have found a new one.

There are also so many elements of the job search that aren't within your control. You can't determine whether relevant job adverts will appear in the newspapers. And neither can you dictate whether networking contacts will put you forward for jobs.

So it's important to focus on the aspects of the job search that are within your control rather than dwelling on the elements that you plainly can't control. Clever clinical psychologists have found that people who tend to spend more time worrying about the uncontrollable factors often experience "learned helplessness." Worry about the uncontrollable makes them prone to lethargy and inactivity. And of course inactivity hardly raises your chances of getting a result. So it creates a vicious circle of inactivity and hopelessness.

One of the best ways to beat "learned helplessness" is to set yourself performance targets and measure your progress. Again, think about it as a vital part of your marketing business plan. After all, a company wouldn't launch a new product without setting goals and checking that it is on course.

Keeping count of your networking encounters is one of the better ways to measure whether you really are spending your time productively or not. It's better than counting the hours you spend in front of your computer writing and rewriting your CV or researching jobs. We all know that it's possible to spend a couple of hours or a whole weekend in front of a computer without accomplishing anything useful. But when we have to speak to someone over the telephone or in person, we tend to be much more alert and more likely to be performing to the best of our ability.

Begin by noting the number of networking emails, phone calls and meetings that you have every day. At first you may be sending out more emails and making only a few phone calls and perhaps attending no meetings at all. But as each day and week passes, set yourself a target and make sure that you achieve it. Spoke to six people yesterday, so need to speak to seven today and eight the next day. Met with five people last week so need to meet with five or even six this week.

Set goals and achieve them. Don't keep putting it off.

UNDERSTAND THE TRUTH ABOUT HEADHUNTERS

A call from a headhunter can seem like a gift from the heavens when it comes to opening up job opportunities. And the marketplace is crammed full of headhunters, recruitment consultants, executive search firms, agencies, and other advisers who claim to be able to help with the job-hunting process. But be careful, as not all so-called headhunters are created equal.

Firstly, remember that just about anybody can set up in business and call themselves a "headhunter" or "executive search consultant." It's pretty much an unregulated industry. And in the absence of regulation, there are as many shoddy and disreputable people around as there are trustworthy and honest ones.

In addition, all headhunters have the same primary goal—which is to keep their clients happy. And while they may address you as if you are the client, bear in mind that the real client is the employer who pays the bills.

"Take a headhunter's advice with a pinch of salt," advises Ian, who recently accepted a leading role within one of the UK's largest media groups. "You can feel that these people are desperate to place you and that the employer really wants you. But bear in mind they are on commission and trade off making money against maintaining important clients, and that might color the extent to which they point out the positives over the negatives of any role you're offered."

Many of the true headhunting firms are paid on a retainer. In other words, they receive a fee for agreeing to take on a search assignment; and they get paid irrespective of whether or not the employer decides to hire any of the shortlisted candidates. However, many of the lesser so-called headhunters and most recruitment consultants are paid on a commission of up to a third of your first year's annual salary. Given that there could be tens of thousands of pounds at stake, there's a huge temptation for the latter category to be prudent with the truth about the job. To some of the least scrupulous firms, you are nothing more than a commodity to be pushed onto employers. Hey, you may end up discovering that you are a square peg in a round hole, but by the time you figure it out, the firm has already cashed the check for placing you.

USE HEADHUNTERS APPROPRIATELY

Given that many headhunters are effectively on commission to place you with their clients, how can you use headhunters without being used? Very simply, when you first have dealings with the firm, ask, "Does your firm do contingency or retained search?"

Firms that work solely on a retained basis will be able to say that they only do retained search work. Firms that work on the basis of contingency fees will typically say that they do both types of work. The answer to this simple question may give you an indication as to the level of trust you might want to place in the advice of the firm.

But even marketing yourself through a retained firm is not without its problems. Even though they are very well connected and can be a key part of your network, relying solely on headhunters and agencies can give you a very limited perspective on the job market. These firms are looking for opportunities with their particular clients. It takes a brave headhunter to suggest that you would be better off applying to an employer that their firm does not represent. So make sure that you use headhunters only as one part of a broader and more proactive search for the right job.

A lot of my headhunting contacts will be having strong words with me for painting such a bleak picture of their industry. And it's true that there are a number of reputable firms and very scrupulous individuals within the industry. But no matter how sincere they seem, remember that they are effectively selling a role to you. So consider their motives with a healthy dose of skepticism. Caveat emptor. Buyer beware!

HUNT THE HEADHUNTER

Job-hunters sometimes wonder what it takes to be headhunted. And of course networking and maintaining a profile among your contacts will help. But the more mundane reality is that even top headhunters are often willing to consider CVs sent to them speculatively.

"The most important thing is to let us know that you exist," advises Ashley Summerfield, at Egon Zehnder International. "Headhunting is often an increasingly inappropriate name for what we do. The process used to be more cloak and dagger—but now there is nothing clever about candidates who make it difficult for us to find them. You should find a firm that you trust and register with them."

On the other hand, the reality is that top headhunting firms get hundreds of CVs.

"Look for warm contacts [within your network]," advises Chris Long, a partner at Heidrick & Struggles. "Try to leverage your way into a business. It's not economically viable for us to see everyone who submits a CV to us—it's just a fact of life. Get a warm contact to introduce you to a search firm."

TARGET THE RIGHT HEADHUNTER

Now you wouldn't try to sell your house through a used car dealership. So why do so many job-hunters try to push their wares on the wrong headhunters?

So don't make the same mistake. Do your homework. Yes there may be certain big brand firms that you have heard of. But are they right for your sector, your role, your level, your background?

If, for example, you have plenty of experience within household name companies, then the top echelon of search firms might be interested. If you have a highly technical background, then there will be certain firms that will welcome people just like you. Or if you have an MBA but less than five years' experience, then a niche firm that focuses on junior management might be better for you.

And get in touch with the right person too. Most of the larger headhunting firms have different practice groups covering specific industries—such as consumer goods, financial services, technology, healthcare, and so on. They may also have functional groupings for finance directors, legal, human resources, supply chain, and so on. The very largest firms may even break practice groups down further into sub-divisions—for example, financial services might be split into banking and insurance subgroups. So you can imagine what will probably happen to your CV if you email it to the wrong person.

Don't just send a CV to the firms that you have heard of. Listen to the grapevine. Ask your network. Which are the best firms for people like you? Whom should you approach within them?

BEWARE OF MATCHMAKERS

Wherever there is money to be made, there will be shady operators. Like sharks sniffing the blood of wounded prey, there are hosts of dubious players ready to pounce upon unsuspecting job-hunters.

Apart from headhunters, there are plenty of career coaches and consultants who claim to be able to take over on your behalf and open up whole worlds of job opportunities for you. And all you need to do is entrust them with a (large) fee.

As a whole, they are an even more questionable lot than even the most unscrupulous of headhunters. Some of the seemingly classier operations advertise in the appointments sections of the Sunday newspapers or the *Financial Times* with straplines screaming "Let us do the work" or "Your time is too precious to waste!"

They may organize seminars or other events and invite speakers from big names in executive search or industry. But it doesn't mean that those speakers or their organizations endorse the matchmaker.

They say that they will write your CV. But why should you pay someone else to write your CV when you are the only person who really knows your most relevant strengths and the weaknesses that you need to be careful of?

They maintain that they will put your CV in front of hundreds of top recruiters. They claim that their sophisticated computer system will identify dozens of perfect opportunities. Or that they will facilitate meetings with senior managers desperate to meet job-hunters just like you. But if they were really so good at what they claim to be able to do, then don't you think you would know someone who had used the services of such a firm?

However, don't confuse these matchmaking businesses with consultants who might be able to offer you specific advice or coaching on particular topics. But always pay for these services on an hourly basis so you know exactly what you are getting. For example, a psychologist might be able to use psychometric tests to analyze and help you understand weaknesses as well as strengths that you might be unaware of. Or perhaps a consultant could help you to sharpen your interview technique.

Never part with a large up-front fee, because the truth is that many of these consultants are usually better at selling themselves and pocketing your fees than they are at selling candidates to employers. Job-hunting can be discouraging if not downright depressing. And these firms' claims of being able to do all of the legwork for you are naturally very alluring. But don't let them take advantage of you in your darker moments.

ACE YOUR EMOTIONS

Of course you know better than to break down in a flurry of tears at an interview or to vent your fury by shouting and screaming at a new contact. But even your suppressed emotions can hamper your efforts to find a job.

The world of work usually veers away from the tawdry business of human emotion. Most managers and professionals know that it could be career suicide to show any hint of negative emotion. Of course, you need to be (or at least pretend to be) positive and upbeat at all times.

But just because you aren't supposed to show your emotions doesn't mean that you don't feel them. And job-hunting can ignite some very powerful emotions—frustration and hopelessness, or even outright anger and depression.

Negative emotions can strip you of your ability to get on with the task at hand. Despondency can rob you of your energy and willingness to approach new contacts; bitterness could leak into your interactions with new contacts, causing them to smile politely at your requests and secretly think to themselves that they would never recommend anyone like you to their contacts.

Don't think that this won't happen to you. Just because you may be intelligent and experienced, a respected professional in your field, you will experience emotional downs as well as ups. But the good news is that I'm not recommending months of lengthy therapy. Simply ACE your emotions:

- Accept your emotions—don't pretend that you are OK. Don't pretend that you don't have bad days. And don't beat yourself up about the fact that you may be feeling angry or unhappy. Accept that it is OK to experience emotions—it's one of the benefits of being a higher life form.
- Capture your emotions—once you've stopped giving yourself a hard time about your state of mind, try to capture what it is that you are feeling. How do you feel and why are you feeling it? A quick trick to shaking off an undesirable emotional state is to write it down. That's why so many people keep diaries— capturing and writing down their feelings helps them to manage them more effectively. So write down the negative emotions that you are feeling and then write five points as to why you should feel good about yourself. I know it sounds more than a little pop-psychological, but trust me because it works.
- Express your emotions—try to talk about your feelings with somebody. In technical parlance, it's known as self-disclosure: disclosing to other people what you are feeling as well as why you feel that way. But I'm not suggesting that you talk to a counselor or a psychologist, a therapist or a psychoanalyst. There's a growing

body of research showing that talking over your emotions with a close friend can be just as beneficial as paying a professional to listen to you. Just make sure that you tell someone—anyone—how you feel.

Don't think of ACE-ing your emotions as an optional extra. It is a vital part of managing your emotions while you network so that you can remain effective in your efforts to find a new job.

BEING
UNFORGETTABLE
AT INTERVIEWS

You're bright, you're good at your job, you're smart, you're confident. You may be socially gifted one-to-one and great at giving presentations to even large groups of people. Perhaps you sell to customers or clients. You may even interview candidates in your role. But none of that means that you will automatically be as good at interviews as you might hope you are. After all, it's a very different story when you are on the other side of the desk.

Most managers and professionals believe that they are good at interviews. Unfortunately, being good at your job is a very different skill from being good as an interview candidate. I've met plenty of candidates who were not as good as they thought they were. And I'm not talking about junior managers or graduates—I'm talking about divisional directors, heads of business units, vice presidents in investment banks, candidates for partnership in law firms, and so on. Senior, experienced people who fell down at the interview stage because they didn't appreciate the rules of the game.

In professional and managerial roles, interviewers are looking for what can effectively be summed up as the "four Cs" of interviewing:

- *Competence*. Being good at the job, which means not only having the right skills and experience, but also being able to share this information—treading the line between providing enough information and being

succinct enough to convince the interviewers
that you're the one for the job.
- *Confidence*. Being self-assured, engaging, and
interesting—but appropriately so.
- *Capacity for growth*. Being able to demonstrate
that you will not only be the right candidate to
fill the vacancy, but also for a longer-term career
within the interviewers' organization.
- *Chemistry*. Having a good interpersonal fit with
the interviewers and what the interviewers
believe to be the culture of their organization.

Make no mistake—interviewing is a game. And,
as in any game, there are rules to be followed. So here
they are.

STAY FOCUSED

Good interviewing begins in your preparation. The first
of the "four Cs" of interviewing refers to competence.
And the way to demonstrate your competence is to
make sure that you have plenty of examples to talk
about how you have exercised the kinds of skills that
the interviewers are looking for.

So read the job advert and try to reconstruct
the job description for the role. What are the handful
of key characteristics and skills that the interviewers
will want to discuss? Even if they are not mentioned
explicitly, what are the implicit qualities that
they want?

If, for example, an advert says that they are looking for a leader to turn around a business, then what stories will you choose to illustrate how you have demonstrated your leadership? You might want to talk about how you have removed under-performers from the team and recruited new people into it. You might talk about the measures that you introduced to improve the situation. Above all, you will need to quantify your achievement by giving some explanation of how you have affected the bottom line of the business, customer satisfaction, the morale of the team, or other measures of performance.

Just as you would never go to an important client meeting without researching the client's needs and thinking about what you want to talk about, make sure that you never become too full of yourself to prepare for interviews.

But be careful not to claim that you are good at everything. If you try to sell yourself too hard, you will come across as pushy and arrogant. So focus on the key skills that the interviewers are likely to be looking for. And don't worry about trying to be perfect at absolutely everything.

GRAB YOUR OPPORTUNITY

"I can usually tell within the first minute whether a candidate is the right kind of person for us," says Warren, owner and Managing Director of a media sales firm. "It's usually something about their manner, bearing, eye contact, and even handshake."

But you know that first impressions count. Everyone makes snap judgments about other people. And there's compelling research showing that most interviewers have a strong idea of whether to reject a candidate within the first ten, five, or even fewer minutes of an interview. The rest of the interview is often no more than a courtesy.

And within those first moments, the nature of your handshake can have a disproportionately large impact on the outcome of the interview. In fact, I know a top lawyer who is quite happy to tell colleagues that she routinely rejects candidates for the limpness of their handshakes. So while it is strange, it is also true that many interviewers like to play pop psychologist when it comes to candidates' handshakes.

A weak handshake or when a candidate proffers their fingers rather than their entire hand has been taken by some interviewers to indicate a feebleness of will as well as grip. An overly strong grip (usually by men) has been read by more than one interviewer as a sign of overcompensation for other weaknesses.

But perhaps the biggest sin is the clammy shake. Save the exchange of bodily fluids for your most intimate encounters—not interviews. So if you're a nervy type whose sweat glands go into overdrive at tense moments, go rinse your hands under a cold tap in the minutes before an interview. Or at least discreetly wipe the palm of your hand on the back of your trouser leg or skirt.

BE CONFIDENT

An American football coach by the name of Vince Lombardi once remarked: "Confidence is contagious; so is lack of confidence."

No prizes for guessing what the second of the "four Cs" stands for then.

Now some readers will have no doubts about their ability to shine in interviews. But if you find that your heart quickens and your breath catches in the moments before an interview, try a little psychological trick to boost your confidence.

Ever tried positive affirmations?

Quite often you may have a niggling voice at the back of your head telling you what might go wrong. But positive affirmations can chase away that inner voice and improve your mood.

Positive affirmations are simply upbeat statements about yourself. They should be statements about what you are or want to achieve as opposed to what you want to avoid. For example, try "I am relaxed" rather than "I am not nervous." And they work simply by convincing your brain that you really are as confident as you tell yourself.

It's one of those tricks that people use but never talk about. One of my clients is an HR Director who has always seemed supremely confident. And when she was forced to look for a new job after her business was acquired by a competitor, she asked for a little support in her hunt for a new job. She surprised me by owning up to using positive affirmations. But she reminded me that just because she always appears outwardly confident doesn't mean that she always feels it inwardly.

As part of your preparation for an interview, think about the right statements for you. What works for someone else won't necessarily apply to you. For example, you might simply repeat, "I am calm, I am confident." Or you might want a lengthier series of statements such as "I have ten years' experience in this field and I am a great manager. I will show my passion for our field and my enthusiasm for this role."

Psychological research shows that an optimistic state of mind can actually lower physiological levels of the stress hormone cortisol. So stress isn't just "in the mind." Chasing away your psychological demons may help to relax you bodily too.

So once you have figured out the statements that work for you, repeat them to yourself in the moments before an interview. Even better, find an empty toilet stall and repeat them out loud. Don't

do it half-heartedly—say them as if you mean them.
Just make sure you don't get caught talking to yourself
in the toilet.

TELL A COMPELLING STORY

The most seemingly innocent of questions can
contain traps for the unwary candidate. Even if the
interview is presented as being an "informal chat,"
make no mistake that your every word, nuance,
and movement are being evaluated. And no more so
than with the popular opening question, "Tell us a
bit about yourself."

Don't make the classic mistake of revealing too
much about your personal life. I've heard too many
candidates start by talking about where they were born
and where they grew up. But do you think interviewers
care where you were born and bred?

And then I've had candidates spend a minute or two
telling me about how proud they are of their children
or the fact they survived a heart attack or gave up
smoking. While none of this is wrong per se, bear in
mind there is an opportunity cost to talking about your
personal life. You are wasting precious minutes that
could be spent talking about the experience and skills
that make you the ideal candidate for the job.

Instead of blurting out your personal life story,
answer this question as if the interviewers had

actually asked: "Tell us briefly about your career highlights, focusing on the last three years and the relevant skills or qualities that should make us pick you for this job." Keep your answer short and to the point—speak for no more than 90 seconds to begin with. After all, an interview is a dialog, not a monolog.

And as this may be the first interview question of the day, are you prepared to make a sterling impression on the interviewers with your response? Do you know which aspects of your career you wish to highlight? Are you totally confident that you will be able to get across your key points without a single "um," "er" or moment's hesitation? If not, take just a few minutes to think about your answer and practice it out loud a couple of times.

DEVISE SEVEN SUCCESS STORIES

I usually recommend that candidates for entry-level jobs try to commit to memory answers to the commonest interview questions. But you're not an entry-level idiot or dummy, are you?

Most interviewers are fixated on achievements and examples of situations in which you took control and delivered results. Unfortunately, there is nothing worse than being unable to recall a specific success or achievement only to remember it days or even moments after the interview has ended. So you might want to spend a little time thinking about your key success stories.

I'm not saying that you need to write out and memorize these stories. But it will help you to sound more fluid and confident if you at least have a rough idea of the tales that you want to tell.

Many large organizations have management competencies—or groups of skills that they believe are critical for success at work. These will differ from organization to organization, but the seven commonest generic managerial and professional competencies tend to cover:

- Analytical and problem-solving skills—being able to assimilate data, evaluate different options and come to a timely decision.
- Communication skills—not only conveying factual information but also rousing and inspiring others, both on a one-to-one basis and with large groups.
- Customer or client skills—winning over new customers and retaining customers.
- Leadership skills—managing a team, delegating work effectively, and handling problems with individuals or, for example, disagreements between individuals.
- Commercial and strategic planning skills— understanding the goals of the organization (typically profitability and shareholder return

in most private enterprises) and being able to organize and drive projects to completion.

- Coaching and development skills—giving constructive positive and negative feedback and helping others to improve their performance measurably.

- Innovation and change skills—generating ideas and turning them into initiatives that have practical benefit for your organization.

So what stories would you use to illustrate each of those competency areas?

Well-trained interviewers tend to shy away from asking about achievements and accomplishments outside of work. However, many line managers who are untrained in interviewing may still ask about successes outside of the workplace. So make sure that you have a few of these to talk about too. But remember that even these accomplishments should in some way show off relevant skills. Perhaps you manage a budget for a local community group or coach children in a sports activity. Don't say that your family is your biggest achievement as that just makes you sound sad. So what are your two biggest achievements outside of work?

SPOT COMPETENCY-BASED QUESTIONS

Heard of competency-based interviewing? To cut a long story short, a bunch of pesky business school professors and psychologists have established that one of the best predictors of future job performance is past performance. So competency-based interviewing tries to dissect your previous experience to scrutinize how you have tackled situations in the past.

Competency-based questions always ask you for actual examples of situations that you have been in. They often start along the lines of "Tell me about a time when you ..." or "Give me an example of a situation in which you ..." or "Can you talk me through an occasion when you ..." and so on.

In answering these questions, always talk in the first person singular about the contribution that you made to a project. So talk about "I did ..." rather than "We did ..." because you need to make it clear the role you played in any situation that you talk about.

At work, we are encouraged to work and think in terms of the team. Many of us have it beaten into our heads that "There is no 'I' in team" (don't trite little management adages like that just make you want to be sick?). But in an interview, remember that the team is not applying for a job. It is you as an individual who is being evaluated. So make your personal contribution very clear to the interviewers.

BE A STAR

Competency-based questions are designed to catch liars out. Just as a police detective fires multiple questions in quick succession at suspects, be ready for the interviewers to probe about your experiences in lots and lots of detail.

Skilled competency-based interviewers tend to make the discussion feel slightly like an interrogation, bombarding you with dozens of questions. Who was involved? What did you do? Why did you do it? How did any other people react? What did you do next? What did they say? How did you react? What was the outcome? What would you do differently?

What the interviewers are trying to determine from the detail of your responses is whether your approach to the situation matches the ideal pattern of behavior that they are looking for.

A little acronym, STAR, might help you to remember the key points that you simply must get across:

- *Situation*—give only a couple of sentences to set the scene.
- *Task*—explain in as few sentences as possible what your role was or goals were in the example.
- *Actions*—spend most of your time describing the actions that you took. And share with the interviewers your thinking processes and the other options you considered. Remember to speak in the first person singular to make your

contributions stand out from those of the other players in your story.
- *Results*—always finish off by quantifying the results that you achieved.

The situation, task, and results are always secondary. It's the actions you took that will make you stand out from the crowd. So make sure that you weight the focus of your examples appropriately.

SNATCH SUCCESS FROM FAILURE

What's the "right" answer when an interviewer asks you about a situation that didn't go as planned? And no, the answer isn't to say that you can't think of one.

Most candidates are ready to talk about situations in which they achieved glowing results. But competency-based interviewers often try to catch candidates out by asking about situations that ended in failure too. "Thank you for that example of how you dealt successfully with a difficult member of the team. Can you now give us an example of a time that did not go so well?"

It's an added question that can flummox many candidates. But the key to talking about failure successfully is to give a further example of a situation in which you did everything possible, but the circumstances or simple blind luck meant that you didn't achieve the outcome that you wanted.

Perhaps a plan was derailed only because of an executive decision taken many levels above you that you could in no way have influenced. Maybe a venture failed to come to fruition because of a crisis elsewhere in the company or the unexpected resignation of key members of the team. Or a project failed to come about because of unforeseen market forces that absolutely no one could have predicted.

So long as you can demonstrate that you took all reasonable actions to try to get an endeavor on track, it doesn't matter that your story eventually ended in failure. Just make sure that you invest a few moments of pre-planning to choose the right examples from your own experience to ensure that you number among those elite candidates who can talk successfully about failure.

COUNT DOWN THE TOP TEN

Interviewers are a fairly lazy breed. Or at least most of them are. But that's good news for you. Because while a few interviewers try to catch candidates out by devising wholly original questions, most interviewers end up recycling the same questions.

Based purely on my personal—but still rather extensive—experience of having sat in on dozens and dozens and dozens of interviews, here is the top ten list of the commonest managerial and professional interview questions:

- "What are your strengths?"
- "What are your weaknesses?"
- "What motivates you?" / "What are you passionate about?"
- "How would your colleagues/boss/customers describe you?"
- "What are your main achievements?"
- "What are your performance targets and how are you doing against them?"
- "What are you most proud of?"
- "Do you have any regrets?"
- "Why should we hire you?"
- "What can you bring to the team?"

The more discerning among you may have noticed that a lot of these questions are very similar. But don't think that you have to give wildly different answers each time. It's more important to stay on message. Think about the key points that you want to make and keep reinforcing them in slightly different ways.

And remember to pick answers that focus on your professional life. You may be terribly proud of your 30-year marriage, your children, or your golfing handicap, but interviewers are unlikely to give you a job because of them.

COMPENSATE FOR YOUR WEAKNESSES

If I had to be honest about my weaknesses, I'd say that I have an incredibly short temper, I'm lousy with numbers, and have poor attention to detail. And I'm actually happy to tell that to interviewers too.

"What are your weaknesses?" is an old favorite question of interviewers. But saying that you have no weaknesses is often taken as a sign of arrogance or a stunning lack of self-awareness and an unwillingness to be self-critical. But neither is total and gushing honesty a good option as listing all of your flaws and imperfections could make you sound, well, weak.

And don't think that you can get away by replying that you are a perfectionist or that you "don't suffer fools gladly." Both of these are clichéd answers that sound more rehearsed than real.

Instead, smart candidates know that they need to divulge some minor weaknesses about themselves. But, again, a little forethought will help you to choose the right weaknesses to reveal. What weaknesses would be acceptable in the particular role for which you are applying? For example, it's OK to mention that you aren't terribly good at attending to detail if you are sure that you will have junior members of the team to handle it for you. Or if your role involves a lot of contact with people, you could say that you have never been very good at working on your own.

Of course, make very certain that the answer you give does not relate to one of the key competencies you have identified for this job.

But those pesky competency-based interviewers sometimes complicate the question of weaknesses further. "Tell us about the last time you received negative feedback? And what did you do about it?" They want to hear about not only your weakness but also the steps that you took to deal with it.

Another popular slant on the question is to ask "Tell us about a personal weakness and how you compensate for it." So make sure that you have an example at the ready to illustrate how you have developed and improved.

DEFUSE PROBLEMS

Many candidates have a specific Achilles heel—some topic that they don't want to discuss, a question that they hope won't get asked. Perhaps you failed an exam somewhere along the line or left an employer under compromising circumstances. Maybe you are simply older or younger than most of the other candidates, or have a visible disability. But what if the question does get asked?

One option is to hope and pray that the question does not get asked. But simply hoping that a question does not come up is hardly the proactive outlook of a smart professional, is it? And worrying about a topic area is not going to help your chances of radiating confidence. So take the time to prepare a few answers.

Review your CV and list the topics that could cause you problems. And then prepare a position statement for each in advance. Work out the precise words that you will use to talk about each issue. Why did you leave that particular company? Why did you not finish a course or pass an exam? How would you feel about us approaching your last boss for a reference?

I normally advise professional and managerial candidates not to memorize interview answers because doing so can make them appear stilted and unnatural. But for any problem areas, it is worth taking the time to prepare a carefully worded answer that you feel comfortable with. Marketing yourself effectively is all about finding the right way to position yourself— were you a victim or the hero in the story? To what extent are you prepared to share the facts, downplay the truth, or even lie? You don't want to have to make that kind of decision on the spot under the pressure of having interviewers drumming their fingers and waiting for your response.

TAKE A PROACTIVE STANCE

As the saying goes, the best defense is a good offense. So sometimes you may need to be more proactive if an issue is more obvious or immediately apparent to the interviewers. You might be considerably older or younger than other candidates, have a visible disability, or be noticeably pregnant. Maybe you have a conspicuous gap in your CV—for example due to lengthy unemployment or a period of illness.

But before you draw the interviewers' attention to the issue, consider whether this is genuinely an issue for interviewers or just an issue for you. You don't want to fall into the trap of raising an issue if it has not actually crossed the minds of the interviewers. For example, age is more often a perceived issue for candidates than interviewers.

But if you are sure that there may be an issue, think about preparing a short statement to deliver proactively. Choose both your words and tone carefully. Would a spot of humor be appropriate? Are facts and reassurance more important? Or should you address the issue as briefly as possible and try to move onto another more positive topic immediately?

Again, preparation is key to ensure that you deliver a compelling answer and remain in full control of not only what you say but also how you come across when explaining your situation.

TALK ABOUT THE LONG TERM

"Where do you see yourself in five years' time?" is another perennial interviewers' favorite. And of course canny candidates know to tell the interviewers what they want to hear. Of course you plan to stick with the organization and progress up the career ladder. No, you don't want to learn all you can and then set up a competing business or move into private equity.

The third of the "four Cs" of interviewing refers to capacity for growth. Even if interviewers do not ask directly about your plans for the future, they are more often than not looking for candidates who can not only meet the requirements of their current vacancy but also grow and develop into making an even more significant difference to their business in the future.

Make sure you can impress upon the interviewers a sense of progression in your career to date. Especially if your CV shows that you have been in the same role for more than a couple of years. Perhaps you are now managing a larger team or have responsibility for more important clients. Maybe you have a larger budget, mastered new techniques or technology. Even if your job title has not changed in five years, make sure you can explain how your role has evolved and grown. Emphasize how you have proactively taken steps to enlarge your role and develop your skill set.

PASS THE PITTSBURGH AIRPORT TEST

The fourth of the "four Cs" of interviewing refers to chemistry. The interviewers want to find someone who has not only the skills and experience, but also the right personality to blend in with the rest of the team and their culture.

Contrast, for example, the styles of a provincial public sector organization and an aggressive American investment bank. The two will tend to want different sorts of candidates. And good candidates know that they need to work to generate chemistry with whatever type of organization they interview with.

I've heard interviewers call it the Pittsburgh Airport Test. Projecting themselves into the future, the interviewers would imagine working on a project with you. Suppose that their connecting flight has been cancelled and that they have 24 hours alone with you until the next flight. Unfortunately, you're stuck at—you guessed it—Pittsburgh Airport. And I bet you can't name three interesting things to do at Pittsburgh Airport. So if they were stuck with you, would they be able to chat happily and kill the time? Or would they end up just wanting to kill you?

At the end of the day, the Pittsburgh Airport Test is about whether the interviewers like you or not. So consider not only what you say but also how you say it.

PLAY THE GAME

Would you burp or fart loudly during an interview? Hopefully not. But why is it then that so many candidates believe that they can just "be themselves" at interviews?

Remember that interviewing is a game. And in this game you have to persuade the interviewers that you are the type of person whom they want to hire. If the interviewers are looking for a certain type of person, then you need to do your utmost to become that person—at least for the duration of the interview.

Some job-hunters see it as an unacceptable level of play-acting or fakery. But the clever candidate merely sees it as presenting different facets of their own personality. After all, you know that the face you present to a client or customer is very different from the face you show your colleagues, which in turn may differ from the one you show your boss. We rarely have the luxury of "being ourselves" with anyone except for our closest friends or family. Different situations merit different behaviors. You wouldn't burp or fart in front of your boss or a client. So why not play down certain aspects of your personality and focus on others during an interview too?

Talk to your contacts and do a bit of research to get an idea of an organization's culture. And pay careful attention to the language and behavior of the interviewers too. Do they describe their organization as being a young and fun place to work?

Do the interviewers exude a confidence that borders on arrogance? Or does the situation require decorum and utter seriousness? Whatever the culture of the organization and the nature of the interviewers, your task is to emulate it.

COMMUNICATE WITHOUT WORDS

Any half-decent candidate knows better than to sit with their arms folded or their legs crossed, because these can be read as signs of defensiveness. And of course you know the importance of making good eye contact to project a confident demeanor.

In fact, some research studies estimate that over half of the impact that people have on each other is derived from the dance of non-verbal cues more commonly known as body language. It really is a case of what you say being less important than how you say it.

So communicate your abject attentiveness by nodding your head and lifting or "flashing" your eyebrows occasionally when the interviewers are speaking to demonstrate your attentiveness. Use the so-called "active listening" technique to signal that you are listening intently to the interviewers' every word.

And don't forget to use the full range of facial expressions appropriately when, for example, talking about a favorite project or a difficult decision. The occasional smile might not go amiss either to show that you are not just a committed professional but also a warm human being.

Use your hands to engage the interviewers visually as well. Research shows that people who gesture with their hands are not only visually more interesting but tend to be evaluated as more credible too. So imagine what hand gestures you would use when talking about how you were forced to take decisive action with a difficult member of your team or when enthusing about why you want to join this particular company. How would you interpret an open palm or a clenched fist? If you don't use your hands naturally, try observing colleagues in meetings and you'll soon identify plenty of hand gestures that you can adopt for your own use.

And think about your posture too. For those moments when you want to emphasize a key point or perhaps hint at the sensitive nature of what you are discussing, try leaning forward and closing the gap between yourself and the interviewers.

Strong interview candidates realize that an interview performance involves more than a touch of theatre. So how will you enrapture your audience and gain rave reviews?

PITCH YOURSELF AT THE RIGHT LEVEL

Passion, determination, and credibility. Interviewers want it all, don't they?

But when it comes to picking from a strong shortlist of candidates, interviewers rarely choose one candidate over the rest because of particular skills and experience. More often than not, it does come down to fairly intangible qualities and characteristics such as passion or even being "leaderly."

So make sure that you deliver your interview responses in the right way. Again, it's a case of how you speak overriding—or at least equaling—the importance of what you speak about.

Unfortunately, too many candidates give no thought to their vocal qualities when it comes to selling themselves at interview. But if the interviewers cannot discern your zeal and inspirational ability in the course of an interview, why should they believe that you could transmit such qualities to their team, customers, or clients?

Now don't think that this can't possibly apply to you. And as we can never hear ourselves as other people hear us—something to do with the Eustachian tube that connects our voice box to our inner ear—can you be 100 percent certain that you are as engaging as you would like to believe?

I'm sure you can think of a number of quite senior people who suffer from flat or lifeless delivery. And they don't think that they are boring either. So don't fall into a smug sense of being good enough.

The only way to know how you sound is to record your voice. Ask a business associate to interview you while you tape the interaction. Of course you must take it seriously and your associate needs to make it challenging for you. And then listen to how you come across.

Do you vary your tone and inflection to match the mood of a discussion or to emphasize particularly important words? Do you modify your volume to convey different emotions?

Consider dropping your voice to a conspiratorial whisper when talking about difficult times or hinting at other people's indiscretions. Think about raising the pitch and volume of your voice when recounting a successful endeavor or imagining a desired goal.

If you are stumped for ideas, try to find role models around you. The next time you are in a group meeting, try looking away from whoever is speaking and listening to the qualities (or lack of them) in their voice. Find a television chat show and listen to the discussion without watching it. Learn from others' mistakes and steal the techniques that you think might work for you.

Listen and re-listen to yourself. And stop only when you think you sound good.

BUILD A SENSE OF GRAVITAS

Qualities such as charisma and gravitas are often bandied around in the workplace. And they can often be created by varying the speed of your speech and using pauses to good effect.

Most candidates allow their interview responses to fall out of their mouths at pretty much the same speed throughout a discussion. For some candidates that speed might be a little faster than normal if they suffer from a touch of nerves or excitement.

But using only the one speed sounds boring. So mix things up a little.

For example, younger candidates who want to be seen as more experienced might think about introducing more pauses between sentences to allow the interviewers more time to ponder on their words. Older candidates might occasionally want to shift into a higher gear to show that they still have the energy to do the job.

Another tip is to try to match the speech patterns of your interviewers. One of the keys to building rapport is that people tend to like people who are like themselves. In other words, interviewers will warm to you more if you seem more like them. I'm not suggesting that you should try to pick up on their accent or turns of phrasing. But if they are speaking quickly and excitedly or slowly and calmly, you might do well do speed up or slow down a little too.

DRESS FOR SUCCESS

Chemistry matters. Often it matters more than competence. And when it comes to gauging chemistry and cultural fit, sometimes the wrong clothes can spoil your chances before you have even opened your mouth to say hello.

It all used to be so much easier in the days before the dot.com boom and bust. The rules of dressing for interviews were simple enough: always wear a suit. But that conventional wisdom doesn't always work these days.

Women tend to suffer at the hands of male interviewers more than the other way around. I've heard men talk disparagingly about women candidates wearing trouser suits, inappropriately low-cut tops or too much jewelry. However, men are not exempt—for example, a survey of US managers found that most interviewers distrust candidates with facial hair.

Basically, clothing and grooming do matter. They shouldn't matter, but they do.

There are interviewers who consider bitten nails to be a sign of lack of willpower on the part of candidates. And interviewers who believe scuffed shoes indicate disorderliness of mind. Of course, any reputable psychologist would tell you that such beliefs are total rubbish—but it doesn't stop line managers from persisting with their strange ideas.

Incredibly, human resources departments even admit in anonymous surveys that, with all other factors being equal, they would prefer not to hire overweight candidates. Now I'm not saying that you should immediately go and try to lose 20 pounds—I'm just informing you because these matters do play on the minds of interviewers whether we like it or not.

To sum up, clothes and your appearance do play a part in the impression that you make. So make sure that you look the part for each and every interview. Not doing it won't get you rejected out-of-hand, but it might be enough to sway the balance subconsciously in the minds of the interviewers. Try to think ahead and try to fit in.

ALWAYS LOOK ON THE BRIGHT SIDE OF LIFE

Interviews are not the right time to be honest. While honesty is an admirable quality, another of the unwritten rules of successful interviewing is to give the impression of being honest rather than actually being too honest.

So try to talk about the positives rather than mentioning the negatives in your career. For example, in answer to the question "Why are you looking to leave your company?" try to talk about what attracted you to the opportunity at hand rather than carping about why you are unhappy in your current job. No one likes a whiner.

Never bitch about a previous employer as it will backfire and reflect badly on you. Or if an interviewer asks you to relate the biggest fault of your current boss, try to respond with some relatively minor flaw before emphasizing qualities of your boss such as how much you learn from them and the amount of autonomy you get in your role.

The same goes for talking about the rubbish team that you have to manage. After all, as the manager, surely it is your responsibility to coach and develop them into becoming a good team. So doesn't admitting to having an inadequate team simply mean that you are a bad manager?

Of course there's a fine line between diversion and evasion. And the latter is something that infuriates interviewers. So be careful and use your judgment.

FOLLOW THE LEADER

Here are some of the stranger questions and requests that I have heard interviewers ask candidates:

- "If you were a letter of the alphabet, what would you be and why?"
- "Who would you rather meet—Albert Einstein or Michael Jackson?"
- "Sell me this angle poise lamp."
- "If you could host a dinner party with any six people living or dead, whom would you choose and why?"
- "Tell me a joke."

Human resources professionals would never dream of asking such weird and wonderful questions. But unfortunately most line managers have never been taught what constitutes effective and professional interviewing. And even when line managers do get taught, they don't always listen. So they continue to ask their idiosyncratic little questions.

But these questions illustrate a more serious point too. Interviewing is effectively a grown-up version of the child's game "Follow the leader." No matter how unusual or completely bizarre the manner of the interviewers, you need to follow their lead. If they decide that they want to fire questions at you in an approximation of a Gestapo interrogation, that's their prerogative. If interviewers want to wax lyrical and do most of the talking, again, that's up to them.

Even if the interviewers' questions and requests cross the line and become slightly inappropriate or mildly offensive, I'd advise that you try to smile sweetly and answer the questions anyway. Some interviewers subscribe to a school of interviewing that tries to rile candidates deliberately, believing that it allows them to simulate some of the pressures that you would face if you were to work for them. It's like stress testing a metal joist before allowing it to be incorporated into the structure of a building. Will you break or can you keep your cool?

So follow the lead of your interviewers. Be adaptable and flexible to the foibles and idiosyncrasies of individual interviewers. Don't rule yourself out of consideration by refusing to play the game. Even if you dislike the interviewers immensely, at least wait until you are offered the job because then you can have the smug satisfaction of turning it down.

HANDLE ILLEGAL QUESTIONS

Interviewers sometimes ask questions that are not just strange or slightly offensive but in fact downright illegal. Increasing employment legislation means that interviewers should not ask questions about marital status, children or the intention to have children, childcare arrangements, religion, place of birth, nationality, sexual orientation, or even age. However, few line managers have much knowledge of or care for employment legislation.

In theory you would be well within your rights to refuse to answer such illegal questions. However, you're not going to get offered the job. You could try to take the employer to court on a count of discrimination—but in practice, discrimination can be tricky to prove. And if the discrimination happened as a result of ignorance rather than a deliberate act of malice, wouldn't you rather just try to get the job?

If, for example, the interviewers ask about your marital status, one tactic would be to decline answering the question and go on to inform the interviewers as politely as possible that it's actually an illegal question.

Another tactic might be to inform the interviewers respectfully that the question is a little controversial. But then go on to answer it anyway. That might demonstrate that while you aren't the kind of person who allows others to push you around, neither do you have anything to hide.

A third option would be to answer the question. Swallow your pride and just answer it, hoping that the interviewers will be able to focus on more important matters.

There is no right or wrong answer when faced with illegal questions. It requires a judgment call on your part. For example, telling one set of interviewers that a question is illegal might embarrass them and interrupt your efforts to build a rapport with the interviewers. On the other hand, standing up for your rights in a calm and civilized fashion might just impress other interviewers and boost their opinions of you.

So consider each situation on its own merits. What works in one interview might not work in another. But whatever you do, just be careful not to let your irritation or annoyance show at being confronted with an illegal question.

DEFLECT QUESTIONS ABOUT MONEY

Money, money, money. Everyone works to earn a living. But another rule of the interviewing game is that you must always say that you are not motivated by dirty, filthy cash. Even if it is your sole reason for getting out of bed in the mornings, at least pretend that it isn't.

For a start, raise the issue of salary and benefits too early and it will make you sound greedy. If you talk about money too soon, you send the message that you are more interested in cash than the intrinsic nature of the job, the brand of the organization, or the culture of the team.

The other reason is simply good sales technique. Think about the sales people you have come across. When trying to sell you a big-ticket item, they don't mention the price immediately. They talk up the features and benefits of their product. They get customers to feel the quality, experience the ride, get to know the product inside and out. And only then does the price comes out.

So don't price yourself out of the equation. If you're more expensive than what the interviewers had in mind, at least let them hear more about your wonderful experience and amazing skill set before hitting them with your price.

Try to put off discussing your package until the interviewers have rejected the other candidates and decided that they want you. Bang. That's the moment that the interviewers switch from being shoppers to buyers. And that's the moment that you gain the leverage to negotiate a better deal. Even if you are more expensive than their original budget, they might be willing to revisit their numbers, maybe slash the Christmas party budget, and squeeze some more cash out for you.

So look for ways to deflect questions about salary without being obviously evasive or difficult. Talk about the importance of finding the right role rather than necessarily more cash. Focus on the challenge or particular development opportunity that draws you inexorably to the role. If you can, name key individuals within the organization whom you are keen to work with or learn from. Or tell the interviewers that the company has a brand and reputation that you find irresistible.

Or, an alternative strategy is to avoid talking about it at all and put it into writing.

"One way of moving off the topic is to prepare a one-page document outlining your current package which you can hand over," advises Suzanne Wood at Heidrick & Struggles. "It avoids having that embarrassing discussion face to face. But if you realize that you may be overpriced for a job, it is worth saying that you recognize the need for flexibility in moving, for example, from the private to public sector."

So skirt around the issue or put it in writing. Or maybe do both. The choice is yours. Choose wisely.

DISCUSS OTHER JOB OFFERS

Envy is a very human quality. Your best friend gets a sporty new convertible and you start to wonder if yours needs upgrading; a colleague gets a promotion and you want one too. And interviewers are no different in wanting what others have. So one way to enhance your desirability in the eyes of the interviewers is to mention any other job offers that you may already be considering.

It's up to you how much to reveal. But less is often more. Try to be at least a little enigmatic about it. Imply that the work may involve work of a strategic nature. Say that you have pledged not to disclose commercially sensitive information about the organization. And then let the interviewers' imaginations conceive of a role that could be much more impressive than the reality of the situation.

But do tell the interviewers if you have undertaken to make a decision about your other offers within a certain timeframe. Ask these interviewers what their realistic timeframe may be and try to collaborate on how you can keep in contention for this job without letting down your other prospective employers.

You might be tempted to bluff as a ploy to boost your credibility even if you don't have another job offer. And yes it is possible to bluff and get away with it. So I'm not saying that you should never bluff. But it is very easy to get caught out too. The interviewers need only ask one too many questions about the nature and timing of your other offer to puncture the charade. So be careful.

ASK KILLER QUESTIONS

Interviews are a two-way process—or so interviewers like to tell candidates. But an interview is rarely the right time to find out what you really want to know about the company. You can do that after you have been offered the job.

No, asking questions at the end of the interview is about impressing the interviewers. Make no doubt that your every question is being evaluated as much as all of your previous answers.

Saying that you have no questions can be fatal. Even if you genuinely feel that the interviewers have covered all of your questions in the course of the interview, it is not good enough. You may as well say that you really aren't that interested in the job or the organization.

But not all questions are good questions either.

"Too many candidates struggle to show knowledge about the company that is interviewing them," says Carol-Ann White, HR Director at LEWIS. "Even for senior candidates such as account directors, they don't know the right questions to ask—such as whether the company is financially stable. When it comes to questions, most candidates lack business acumen and research skills."

So while your questions should be positioned as making up your mind about working for the business, the real aim of your questions should be to demonstrate your knowledge and interest in the right aspects of the organization.

For junior roles, stick to questions about the nature of the job itself. Ask about the composition of the team, immediate and longer-term challenges facing the team, and how the vacancy has come about. How much autonomy would you have to shape and restructure the team? What targets would the organization set you and how would your performance be measured?

For more senior roles, ask about the strategy and direction of the organization to show that you are a "big picture" thinker. Ask about the company's plans for the future. What new products or services are being planned? Any large-scale change initiatives? What are the key priorities of the organization over the next 12, 18, or 36 months? You could also try to use your knowledge of the organization and its positioning with regard to competitors to show that you have done your research. For example, given that company ABC has announced its intentions to move into a new field, how has this organization chosen to respond?

Never allow yourself to smile meekly and say that you have no questions. Use questions to demonstrate your interest in the job and show off (subtly) your research and knowledge about the business.

ASCERTAIN THE KEY DELIVERABLES

So you think that you're good at interviews? Want to try a technique that will seal the deal and get you the job?

The very best candidates manage to turn formal interviews into informal discussions. They change the purpose of an interview from being an evaluation of their credibility as candidates into a collaborative discussion about how they and the interviewers would work together to achieve the organization's goals.

And if you are confident that you have mastered the essentials of good interviewing, you could try it too.

As you ask more and more questions of the interviewers, try to get an idea of what the employer is looking to achieve by filling this vacancy. If the job advert mentioned a "turnaround," then what exactly needs turning around? What went wrong in the past? If the organization is "growing," then what kind of growth targets are they looking for within the next few quarters or years?

Ask a few carefully chosen "What?" questions to make sure that you understand their situation, goals, and methods. What has worked in the past? What hasn't worked? What have the obstacles been? What is the situation with other stakeholders across the organization? What are the key deliverables in the job?

However, be aware that the interviewers may not want to tell you the answers. So always preface delicate questions by saying something along the lines of: "I realize that may be sensitive information, but would you mind if I asked about ...?"

When you have a solid grasp of their issues and key deliverables, you can try to nudge the discussion onto how you would tackle those issues and achieve those deliverables.

Make tactful suggestions and offer brief examples from your own experience of how you have overcome similar challenges. But be careful to pitch your ideas as if you were having a team discussion with two colleagues. Don't sell your achievements too hard or you will break the illusion that everyone in the room is joining forces to realize the organization's goals. Treat it as a brainstorming session/workshop as if you have already assumed the role.

It's a tricky technique and some interviewers may be reluctant to relinquish enough control of the interview to allow you to use it. But when it works, you may just reach interview nirvana.

MAKE A LAST-DITCH ATTEMPT

Interviews can be rather like a game of poker. Interviewers usually try their best to put on their poker faces, keeping their emotions and reactions firmly in check. But they aren't perfect at it and sometimes you might get the definite impression that your chances are fading fast.

Perhaps the interview is coming to a close in significantly less time than was scheduled. Maybe it's just a sideways glance between the interviewers or the atmosphere seems distinctly cool. Often the signals are very subtle. But if you are certain that the interviewers are not warming to you, you may have little to lose by changing tactic dramatically.

Rather than following the lead of the interviewers, try to take control of the situation. Anne, a solicitor who had recently left a large law firm, was looking to move into an in-house role within the pharmaceutical sector. In one interview, she took a gamble and offered to work for the company on a trial basis. She told the interviewers that she was so convinced that she wanted to work for this business because of its culture and reputation that she would be willing to come in for an entire week—and work for free.

That was two years ago and she's still working there.

However, bear in mind that this is a high-risk gambit. It's a fine line to tread between being assertive and aggressive, between courage and confrontation. But if you are certain that an interview is not going your way, what do you have to lose?

EXPLOIT THE RECENCY EFFECT

Ever heard of the recency effect? Well, it's just the opposite of the primacy effect, if that helps.

We all know that first impressions count. Good or bad, interviewers are prone to making up their minds very quickly about candidates—which is otherwise known as the primacy effect. Interestingly enough though, last impressions count too—and no prizes for guessing that one is called the recency effect.

There's a big fat body of research showing if you have an hour-long interview, the interviewers will remember most clearly the first handful of minutes but then possibly let their attention wander a bit in the main body of the interview. But then they tend to wake up again and pay more attention as the interview draws to a close.

And in those closing minutes, none are more important than the final few seconds. So make sure that you leave on a high note. Think about the last words that you want to leave the interviewers with. Shift your non-verbal communication into a high gear—big smiles, unwavering eye contact, strong handshake.

You probably have time to utter no more than a sentence or two. So tell the interviewers how much you have enjoyed meeting them and reaffirm your enthusiasm and interest in the role. Or perhaps remind them of the one key fact that you feel may make the critical difference.

Don't let yourself down at the final hurdle.

PREPARE FOR APTITUDE TESTS

Interviewers don't always play nice. And there isn't much nastier play than being subjected to a battery of psychometric tests.

Aptitude tests are supposed to measure essential workplace skills such as your grasp of numbers, your flair with complex verbal arguments, or logical reasoning and problem-solving ability. The theory is that they can't be faked. There are very definitely right or wrong answers. And so these tests allow interviewers to compare candidates in very quantifiable terms.

Of course interviewers should never make decisions based solely on the basis of good or bad test scores. But then again, many do.

Only 11 out of 20? Oh dear, that candidate must be a bit average then. And we don't want average in our organization, do we?

So don't let poor aptitude test scores ruin your chances. Grab a book aimed at helping smart business types like you get to grips with aptitude tests. If you haven't come across one, try a GMAT (Graduate Management Admission Test) book. Flex those mental muscles and get them back into shape.

Okay, you may already remember the difference between an analogy and a simile; you may be able to work out the circumference of a circle. But how quickly can you do it when the clock is ticking and the pressure is on? So get practicing—it could be the difference between being strictly average and top of the class.

BE CAREFUL ON PERSONALITY TESTS

You've probably heard the old cliché that "there are no right or wrong answers" when completing a personality test, right?

Wrong.

In an interview situation, of course the interviewers believe that certain personality traits are more desirable than others. For example, it doesn't take a rocket scientist to work out whether most interviewers prefer extroverts or introverts for managerial and professional jobs.

But be careful trying to lie. Most personality tests have built-in social desirability scales designed to catch out fakers. Personality tests usually ask you to rate the extent of your agreement or disagreement with dozens or hundreds of statements. And it is the statements that contain the words "never" or "always" that often try to trap candidates who are trying to fake socially desirable answers—for example "I am never late for work" or "I am always conscientious in the workplace." Ticking too many such socially desirable statements implies that you may have tried to misrepresent yourself.

Without lying, you can still present yourself in the most positive light by following some simple guidelines. To begin with, people are often different in their home life than they are at work, so always think about how you behave in a professional context when ticking those boxes.

And don't be too self-critical when answering test questions. Try to think about how you typically or ideally like to deal with different situations as opposed to obsessing about whether you always manage to think or behave that way at work. Even the designers of personality tests concede that their tests can only measure how candidates like to behave as opposed to how candidates actually do behave. So if you are wavering between two options on any particular question, give yourself the benefit of the doubt and select the more positive response.

Never try to cheat on a personality test. But perhaps complete it seeing yourself as your mother or best friend might rate you.

KEEP THE MOMENTUM GOING

When was the last time you received a hand-written letter or thank-you note? Probably been a while, hasn't it? So make one final attempt to make a favorable impact on the interviewers.

The interviewers may take a couple of days to make up their minds. So write them a one-page letter summarizing the two or three key points or issues that you feel make you a strong candidate for the job. Keep it short. Keep it punchy. Perhaps you didn't explain yourself as clearly regarding one of your examples. Or maybe you want to add any points that you forgot to mention during the course of the interview. Think about matching the tone of the letter to the tone of the interview too—will you choose to be factual and assertive or introduce a touch of self-deprecating humor?

Even if a follow-up letter does not help you to secure a particular job, it can serve a purpose. It may be the case that another candidate got the job because they were marginally stronger than you in some area. But it doesn't mean that the interviewers thought that you were a weak candidate. Writing a letter keeps you in their minds for a little longer. And that extra reminder might just encourage them to propose you for another job in their organization.

Consider the cost-benefit of writing a follow-up letter. Fifteen minutes—that's all it should take you.

And the cost of some stationery and a stamp. But the pay-off? Well, that could be huge.

BRIEF YOUR REFEREES

When Nikhita was fired from her job as head of the sales support team at a healthcare business, she was more than a little relieved to get away from what she described as "an atmosphere of spitefulness and intimidation" encouraged by her boss. Unfortunately, it left her in a tricky position, as she knew that a reference from her boss would almost certainly be worded to scupper her chances in future jobs.

Your references are as much a part of your marketing campaign as your CV or your interview preparation. And while most candidates are diligent in managing their CV and interview preparation, it's surprising how many candidates don't manage their references unless they are forced to do it.

One of the keys to managing your references is not to include them on your CV unless you are specifically asked to do so. Removing them from your CV means that you at least know when an employer wants to speak to a referee, which allows you a modicum of influence over their discussion.

Of course you can't control everything that your referees say about you. But you can at least make suggestions and point them in the right direction.

Whenever an employer asks to check your references, try to pick the two or three referees who would be most relevant for helping you to secure this particular job. After all, you customize your CV for different audiences, so why not select different referees to vouch for different aspects of your working life? For example, a client may be able to talk about your pitching or negotiation skills, while a colleague might be more able to judge your ability in leading the team. So pick the people who might reinforce the messages you want to send to a prospective employer.

Always brief your referees on the nature of each particular job. Tell them about the chief qualities the employers may want to go into. Remind your referees subtly of particularly poignant examples of when you demonstrated particular skills. If you know your referees well enough to trust in their unequivocal support, then you might also warn them of any issues or doubts that the interviewers may have raised about you.

Going back to Nikhita's situation, she chose to get a reference not from her direct manager but from the sales director with whom she had good relations. It was a slightly risky tactic, as she had to hope that her future employers would not ask about the precise reporting relationship between herself and her referee. But it worked.

Remember that job offers are usually made "subject to satisfactory references." So make sure that your references are satisfactory. But be careful of exaggerating or lying about your experience. Or, if you do exaggerate, at least make sure that your referees are able to corroborate your story!

SOLICIT CANDID FEEDBACK

In the aftermath of an interview, receiving a letter rather than a phone call from the employer is rarely a good sign. The letter may thank you for your interest and express how impressed they were with certain of your skills or experiences, but it all amounts to the same thing: rejection.

Rather than dismiss the experience and move on, it's important to review what happened. In marketing terms, it's like conducting a spot of market research. You launched the product, got a customer to try it out. Unfortunately they didn't like it—but why?

Interviewers frequently tell candidates that another candidate got the job because they had better skills or experience. But they often say that because interviewers hate giving negative feedback to unsuccessful candidates. It's an easy option for them to avoid having to engage their brains and offer up any real criticism.

So you need to seek the equivalent of a slap in the face or a poke in the eye with a sharp stick. Speak with the interviewers and ask for their honest opinion. The key here is not just to get warm platitudes but incisive and insightful feedback—even if hurts.

Use all your powers of influence and persuasion to convince the interviewers to give you candid feedback. Tell them that they are entitled to their point of view. Promise that you will not try to contradict them or change their minds at this stage of the process. Reassure them that you will not get defensive. Tell them that it's the negatives rather than the positives that you want to hear. Explain that any small nugget of constructive criticism would be beneficial.

Of course you mustn't get defensive. Or contradict the interviewers. Or try to change their minds. Because the first hint that you are trying to do any of these things will scare the interviewers off.

Do whatever it takes short of bursting into tears and begging to find out what you could have done better. Think about open-ended questions and more specific questions to prompt the interviewers. Ask what it was that the successful candidate said or did that gave them the edge over you. Use your ingenuity and work out your plan before you pick up the telephone.

It almost goes without saying that you need to learn from the interviewers' comments. Remember that if one set of interviewers has a set of opinions or views about you—no matter how strange or untrue—then it's possible that other interviewers might feel the same way too.

SUSTAIN YOUR EMPLOYABILITY

A few lucky job-hunters can find themselves jumping into a new job with hardly any effort. But most job-hunters say that it takes them anywhere from between a couple of months to many months to find a new job. Occasional surveys report that up to around a quarter of job-hunters can still be looking six months after they started—although it can be much longer for some job-hunters, depending on the health of their sector and the current phase of the economic cycle.

If you find that you are still unemployed three months after your last job has stopped paying you, it may be time to take some steps to prepare for the disagreeable possibility that you may be waging a lengthier campaign than you would like.

Of course a job could be waiting just around the corner. And three months does not seem very long to wait. But what you don't want to happen is to keep waiting until you find yourself still unemployed nine months or a year later without having gained any qualifications or experience at all.

While it's true that there is less of a stigma attached to redundancy than there was twenty or even ten years ago, most employers do still worry about skill atrophy— that a spell of unemployment can dull a person's capabilities or reduce their commercial instincts. So don't let your time go to waste.

At the three-month mark, think about your Plan B. Would it boost your employability to do some form of study? If necessary, could you conceivably position your period of unemployment as having taken time off to gain a qualification?

Or think about getting some form of work. You might easily be able to find temporary employment. But remember that there may be a trade-off between earning money in the short-term and longer-term employability in your chosen field. Some roles might pay the bills but give you little to write about on your CV. On the other hand, a carefully chosen voluntary position might earn you little more than your travel expenses but provide you with weightier, career-building experience. Don't automatically plump for a voluntary position in a large well-known organization because it is easy. Seek out the smaller, unknown organizations that allow you to make a greater impact. Even just a day a week in the right kind of role might be better than five days a week doing the wrong kind of work.

Don't just assume that a job will come your way. No one owes it to you to find you a job. You are the only person who can find one. And just as a good marketing business plan will include best- and worst- case scenario projections, you need to consider a range of job-hunting scenarios. So—at the three-month mark—what are you going to do to maintain your employability?

SIGNING ON THE DOTTED LINE

Congratulations and champagne all around! The first thing to do when you get offered a job is go celebrate. Out of all the many, many candidates who applied for the job, you are the one to whom the interviewers have decided to offer the job.

But don't let your delight cloud your judgment. Employers are in the business of selling their organization to candidates too. And most employers highlight the positives and play down the negatives to some extent. So make sure you weigh up the job carefully and consider whether it really is the right move, not only for now, but also in building your longer-term career.

And then there's the issue of money. Surveys repeatedly show that you will get the largest pay rises when you change jobs. That's the time when you have the most leverage—before you sign on the dotted line. Once an employer has got you working for them, you can expect the situation to change considerably—and not in your favor. So it's a case of now or never in negotiating the best possible deal.

Most organizations will expect you to negotiate. Large organizations often impose salary restrictions that line managers are not supposed to exceed, but interviewers can and do break the rules for exceptional candidates. Small companies may have no such rules. And the more senior the role, the more freedom the organization will typically have to enhance the value of a package to secure the best candidate.

So make sure that you do not end up kicking yourself for not doing your due diligence to ensure this really is the right job for you and then negotiating a great deal.

DEFER SPONTANEOUS JOB OFFERS

It doesn't happen often, but interviewers can be so bowled over by your interview performance that they might just decide to offer you the job there and then. Perhaps the rapport was perfect or your manner and responses met the interviewers' every requirement. Whatever the case, well done.

But don't accept the job. Even if you are certain that this is the job for you, accept the job on the spot and you will compromise your ability to negotiate a better deal.

Do convey your amazement and enthusiasm to be offered the job. Even if you have doubts about whether this is the right job, now is not the right time to express them. At least behave as if you are incredibly pleased and excited to be offered the job.

Then explain that you would obviously like to see a written offer and contract before accepting. The interviewers will appreciate your caution—that you're not the kind of person who makes rash decisions.

Just make sure that you do not say yes!

MEASURE YOUR WORTH

Successful negotiations—much like successful interviews—are often achieved through hard work and preparation beforehand rather than during the discussion. And when it comes to negotiating salary, you really cannot have enough benchmarking data about your comparative worth on the market.

You may never reveal the extent of the information that you hold. In fact, sharing too much information during negotiations may weaken your position. But knowing your comparative worth may allow you to judge how strongly to push and when to back down.

If you have been diligent about establishing a wide network of contacts, then go back to them for information about salary ranges. When you receive a firm job offer, it makes it much easier to go back to contacts with a specific question. Explain that you have an offer and are now trying to negotiate the best deal. Ask about salary and bonuses, perks and other benefits to ensure that you get a total picture of the value of packages at other firms.

If you have a good relationship with an executive search consultant, ask for their advice too. Look back at adverts for other jobs that you applied or considered applying for. Use the wondrous tool that is the internet to get a wider perspective on the issue too.

Bear in mind that you may be able to command more of a pay rise if you are currently employed than if you are not employed. Having job offers from other prospective employers will help to boost the premium that you can ask for too.

Working out your worth is more an art than a science. Establishing that an employer's offer is toward the bottom of the salary range may be more useful than finding out that you are already being offered a package toward its top end. But at the end of the day you are worth what an employer is willing to pay you. So the next step is to think about how to persuade the employer that you are worth just that little bit more.

DETERMINE YOUR OBJECTIVES

Now, you might think that the objective of your negotiation is pretty obvious—namely to get as much as you can. And most candidates simply want the biggest salary that they can agree on.

But employers are remarkably reluctant to part with cash. They may try to offer all sorts of other benefits and incentives instead. So consider other options you might be willing to accept in lieu of hard cash; think about elements of the total package such as:

- sign-on bonuses or allowances for relocation
- commissions, incentives, stock options, profit-shares, and other forms of after-the-fact bonuses

- benefits such as pension, medical and dental cover, life assurance, and sickness and disability insurance
- number of days' annual leave, maternity/paternity allowances, and personal days
- personal development budgets or financial assistance for pursuing further qualifications
- a company car, car allowance, or season ticket loan
- gym memberships and personal expense accounts
- flexible working arrangements such as part-time working, job share or being able to work from home.

Make it a priority to ask for a copy of the employee handbook, as some of the more basic policy issues may be covered in it, helping you to avoid having to go back to the employer repeatedly with questions over the more minor points of your package.

FOCUS ON YOUR PRIORITIES

Negotiations are often seen as nose-to-nose confrontations and a battle of wills. But salary negotiation should never be a case of pushing and pushing in the hopes that the employer will capitulate and agree to your demands.

Negotiations are a process of give and take, of proposals and concessions.

Push too hard and you could end up with a reputation for yourself as difficult to work with before you have even started the job. Even worse, the employer could decide that you just aren't worth the bother and opt for the next strongest candidate instead.

So try to separate out in your mind what you want as opposed to what you need. While it's easy to have a wish list of what you would like, what is the more realistic list of priorities that you simply must have? Don't be afraid to aim high, but always read the tone of the negotiation and be prepared to back down.

For example, one job-hunter in the manufacturing sector was facing the prospect of making a significant loss on the value of his home so was determined to negotiate a relocation package that would cover it. To his surprise, he got it.

As another example, another job-hunter was offered the opportunity to relocate from a job in London for a bigger role working for a South African business in Cape Town. But with currency fluctuations he was worried about the spending power of a South African salary should he ever return to the UK. What he wanted was to be paid a salary in British pounds. But what he was willing to accept (and got) was a pension contribution in British pounds.

Think broadly. Be creative.

If an employer can't offer you the salary that you want, would you be prepared to accept a lower salary with a guaranteed bonus subject to hitting certain performance targets? Or if the employer seems unwilling to offer the salary that you want, would they be willing to give you a 90 percent contract that allows you to take every other Friday off?

Another tip is to ask for phased payments. If they won't give you all that you want in terms of salary, then perhaps agree to a lower initial salary followed by a guaranteed pay rise three or six months down the line.

There are many options to consider. So think ahead and be ready to be flexible in your discussions.

MAKE THE EMPLOYER DO THE TALKING

Negotiations are like a game of poker. Rather than revealing your hand too quickly and saying what you want, see what the employer is willing to offer first. Their offer might well exceed what you had planned to ask for.

Always let an employer be the first to broach the subject of money. When they do bring up the topic, try to make the employers do more of the talking.

The more they talk, the more you learn.

Once they do make an offer, take your time in considering it. Allow a silence to develop. Most people find silence uncomfortable and the employer may break first and offer to raise the offer.

When you do speak, keep your cards close to your chest. Reiterate your interest in the job and the organization, but ask whether there might be room for improvement on the figure. Ask questions that force the employer to keep talking. Information is power and finding out more about the employer's position will allow you to direct your comments and questions accordingly.

Keep asking questions about the different elements of the package. But be careful not to imply that any particular part of the package might be acceptable. It's difficult to backtrack once you have agreed to a figure. Wait until you have an understanding of everything that is on offer before agreeing on any of the individual elements.

A lot of job-hunters don't like to negotiate. Hell, I don't like to negotiate. It feels awkward and I go cherry-red having to ask for more. But maintain a friendly and tactful tone. And so long as you avoid implying any sense of entitlement and reaffirm your interest in the role, you should be able to negotiate a better package than you might otherwise imagine.

ESTABLISH THE PARAMETERS OF THE JOB

Money isn't everything. And most job-hunters agree that they would happily take a pay cut for the right role. So it's worth spending a little time in the course of the negotiation checking that this really is the right job for you.

You should already have a fair idea of the main tasks to be achieved once you take on the role. But think about other parameters of the role too.

Are you happy that you understand your line manager? Do you think that you have a good grasp of his or her management style and personal foibles? There may be limited scope to change line managers, but it isn't completely unheard of to be able to do so provided that you can justify it.

Ask also about any "dotted line" reporting relationships to other people across the business. Especially in large, international organizations, it's not uncommon to find that you may effectively have two or three bosses with competing agendas.

In running the team, ask about the size of the team and the budgets you may control. What scope do you have to hire and fire or otherwise restructure your team?

On a more practical note, when do they expect you to start? Does their start date allow you enough time to get your affairs in order or even to have a holiday before getting to grips with the role?

When it comes to negotiating, don't forget that there are other issues to discuss other than pay and benefits. At the end of the day, you must be completely happy with the day-to-day reality of your role. So are you totally, completely, and resolutely happy?

AGREE CLEAR PERFORMANCE CRITERIA

Deciding to join a new organization should hopefully be the start of a fulfilling and mutually beneficial relationship. Or that's the goal anyway. The reality doesn't always work out that way.

Laura, an audit manager, joined the consumer goods practice of an accountancy firm. She said that she got on "fabulously" with everyone she met during the interview process. And she agreed to accept a starting salary equal to what she was already earning in return for a pay rise six months later contingent on satisfactory performance. When it came to her six-month evaluation, everyone lauded her contributions to the business, but unfortunately her boss said that he had been expecting a little more from her and denied her the pay rise. Laura was of course furious but—without wanting to establish a reputation as a bitter employee who seeks litigation at the first sign of trouble—she had to put up with it.

Such stories are not uncommon. A fair chunk of relationships that break down between employee and employer come down to differences in their expectations. Canny job-hunters therefore know to discuss and agree on a concrete set of performance criteria that—as far as possible—remove the element of subjectivity from the equation.

Remember that you have little or no leverage to seek pay rises, promotions, or further bonuses once you are in the job. So try to tie advancement opportunities to measurable performance criteria such as increases in sales revenue or volume, productivity or profitability. If the organization uses a balanced scorecard, then it might be possible to link your performance to measures such as customer satisfaction or turnover or even employee morale. And if your role is of significant strategic importance, then even market share gains or the capture of key client accounts might be relevant.

Be aware that your ability to negotiate complex deals does depend considerably on the seniority of your role. A graduate or junior manager attempting to seal a complex deal would be laughed at. A senior manager or executive entering the business would not be expected to do otherwise. So use your common sense to avoid spoiling the relationship with the employer before you have even begun your job.

ENSURE A SAFE LANDING

Imagine spending a couple of months on a beautiful Caribbean beach. Employers never mention certain benefits; but canny employees know to pursue them anyway.

Chief among these is the "golden parachute"—a pay-off should the employer want or need to get rid of you. When you have discussed and agreed all other points and criteria, make a sensitive enquiry about the company's severance policy. In some cases, this may already be discussed in the employee handbook.

Then try to negotiate a longer notice period or a payout should the worst happen and the employer needs or wants to get rid of you. Employers often prefer to pay staff to leave immediately rather than ask them to serve their entire notice periods. So agreeing a longer notice period could well be the difference between a relaxed Caribbean holiday and having to scrabble immediately for a new job.

A lot of job-hunters feel reluctant to negotiate over the details of their notice period or severance package—it's too much like asking one's betrothed to sign a pre-nuptial agreement. They say that it's hardly a sign of trust. But employers expect to enter into such discussions with experienced managers and professionals. And so long as you emphasize that it's a precaution that you hope never to need, most employers are more than comfortable to discuss such arrangements.

However, never talk about a longer notice period as a benefit—always position it as a safety cushion on the off-chance that the working relationship goes wrong.

BEWARE OF THE SMALL PRINT

"Even at a senior level, you find that some candidates don't negotiate until after they have signed on the dotted line," says Nicola Forristal, HR Director at BBH. "We try to be transparent, but you as an individual have to open your eyes, read carefully and have the confidence to request further documentation. Some candidates worry about being a pain in the arse, but you don't have to be aggressive about it."

So make sure to ask for everything that has been agreed to be put into writing. The reality of job-hunting in modern times is that jobs rarely last for a lifetime, which makes it critically important to ensure that you will be able to leave this organization—whether it is in 12 months' or 12 years' time—without hindrance.

If you are in a higher salary bracket, it might also be worth seeking the services of an employment lawyer to check the details of the contract for you. If they can find and close loopholes in your contract that might otherwise cost you money, their fee may be well worth paying.

Look out for non-compete agreements too. They are often incorporated as clauses in employment contracts but can also be separate agreements. They may prohibit you from seeking employment from a related organization in your field for a certain length of time. Such agreements may also prevent you from approaching the organization's clients or customers for a number of years. All in all, they can cause major headaches for even junior or mid-level managers seeking to pursue available opportunities.

In reality, non-compete agreements can be difficult to enforce, as some courts perceive them as unfair attempts to limit a person's ongoing ability to seek further employment. But rather than relying on a judicial process to protect your ability to work should you leave this organization, you might be better off asking your employment lawyer to help you keep its terms manageable.

LOOK BEFORE YOU LEAP

There's a big difference between having a succession of jobs and building a successful career. And the more senior you become, the more employers will want to see a logical progression in your career moves.

Paul, a finance director, was made redundant as a result of a restructure at a large telecommunications company. With a mortgage and the expense of two children in private education, he needed to get a job as quickly as possible. "Initially I was keen to move into consumer goods or the media industry. But I listened to advice that it would be difficult for me with 12 years' experience in telcos. I didn't get many interviews and I got knocked back every time. So I took another position in a telco. But I'm only 42 and I know that the next time I look for a job, my chances of changing sector will go from poor to impossible."

Make sure you do not jump into a new role without thinking through the long-term career consequences of your decision; make sure you can satisfy yourself on the following questions:

- To what extent does the role fit into your original vision of what you wanted from your next job?
- Do you have an affinity for this sector? To what extent does the thought of working with this organization's products or services excite you?
- What opportunities for advancement are there within this organization? Or if this is a stepping stone in furthering your long-term career goals, what skills or experience will this add to your CV?
- Do you feel that the role will be stretching and enjoyably challenging? Or will it be insufficiently stimulating and tedious, or even too demanding and stressful?
- To what extent does the brand or reputation of the organization add value to your CV?

- Are the office location and travel requirements of the job acceptable?
- What consequences will this job have on your work–life balance, and your family or other personal relationships?

DO YOUR DUE DILIGENCE

Interviews involve all manner of tricks and fakery—and not just on the part of candidates keen to sell themselves. Interviewers are often just as eager to sell their organization to lure the very best candidates.

"Jobs are rarely what they seem," warns Rod, who previously worked in a senior sales role for a privately owned automotive business. "Everyone throughout the interview process seemed absolutely fantastic—fun, engaging, smart, focused. But if I'd known that the chairman was married to one of the other directors and that there were so many personal relationships, rivalries, and political factions, I would never have joined."

Do not take anything for granted. When considering whether to join a new organization, you are the only person who can establish whether the fit is right for you or not. Even relatively minor issues can become incredibly frustrating if you are used to other working practices—for example a certain level of secretarial or IT support.

Linda, an HR director, left one international listed business to join another international listed business. "I made certain assumptions—I didn't ask questions such as 'how advanced is your IT?'" she admits. Linda is now looking for yet another new role. "But because I didn't do my due diligence, I was incredibly frustrated when I arrived that the new business didn't even have an intranet."

Ask and ask some more. When it comes to deciding about a new job (and once you have a firm offer), almost no question is too stupid. The old adage that "assume makes an ASS out of U and ME" can ring true even for quite experienced job-hunters.

CONSIDER CULTURE CAREFULLY

Once you have a firm offer on the table, you can ask much more probing questions. What is the culture like? How do things really get done?

But while you may ask questions of the interviewers, you are unlikely to get even close to the truth. Interviewers can always choose to tell you what they want you to hear. Or they may simply have no objectivity about the culture that they have now grown so used to.

But there may be other ways to tap into the dark secrets of the organization's real culture.

"Cultural issues are often boss-related," maintains Chris Long at Heidrick & Struggles. "Candidates often say that they didn't realize the boss was like that. Get opinions from other members of the team. Ask why the vacancy has arisen in the first place. And use your network to speak to others who have worked there."

So don't rely solely on the interviewers' or your prospective line manager's opinion. Ask to meet members of the team outside of the workplace. Offer to take your prospective colleagues out for lunch or a drink. But do it one-on-one. Take them out of earshot of other colleagues and ply them with drink. Encourage them to do away with the party line and you might just get at observations that more closely approximate the truth.

Here's a selection of some of the better questions I have heard job-hunters ask:

- How would you describe the culture of the organization?
- What's the best thing about working in the organization?
- Just between the two of us, what frustrates you most about working here?
- Who are the key decision-makers that I will have to interface with? How would you describe their personal style?
- How do decisions get made here? How important is informal networking and influence versus use of formal channels?
- How much do people socialize together outside of work? What was the last social event you went to?

- Why do people typically fail in this organization? What did they do or say?
- Across the team, what differentiates the people who succeed from those who don't?
- To what extent do people work in close teams or autonomously on their own?
- How long do people tend to stay within the organization?
- Do people tend to get promoted from within or brought in externally?

CONCLUDE THE JOB-HUNT

Ultimately, you are the only person who can decide whether a job is for you. Ideally, you would be able to answer yes to both of the following two questions:

1. Would you enjoy all aspects of the job?
2. Would this job help to further your career rather than simply paying the bills?

Hopefully the answers to both questions will be yes. But the unfortunate reality is that some job-hunters are forced to accept less-than-perfect jobs to earn a living.

Whatever the case, don't forget to get in touch with everyone who helped with your job search and share your news with them. Let them know of your new job title, the role, and a little about the organization. Make sure that they have all of your new contact details too. Hopefully you won't need to draw upon the support of your network in finding a new job for some years, but they are a valuable resource that you should never neglect.

Show your appreciation as appropriate depending on their level of contribution to your job-hunt. For some it might be a call or just an email. For others, it might be a handwritten note or even flowers. For the few that deserve the extra credit, dispatch a bottle of wine or offer to buy them a lavish meal. But let everyone know how much you valued their support during the job-hunting process.

Congratulations. And enjoy your new job!

FINAL THOUGHTS

You can find a new job. One that is more enjoyable, more aligned with your skills and interests, and of course better paid too.

I coach so many job-hunters who stumble because they don't understand the new rules of getting a new job. So what are the biggest mistakes – and how can you avoid them?

When it comes to applying for jobs, most job-hunters jump straight to the stage of sending out applications or CVs. They don't put the thought into exactly what they want. Most job-hunters simply look for work that is similar to what they were last doing or are currently doing. But you. You will think about your core skills and interests. You will think about the kind of work that most appeals to you, so you can go to employers full of fire and motivation about the work you really want to do. Already, by being truly motivated about your work, you will stand out from the crowd.

When it comes to sending out those applications, most other job-hunters fall into the trap of updating an old CV rather than creating a new one. Oh dear. But, of course, you won't make that mistake. You will create a CV from scratch, carefully selecting the right information that is guaranteed to make employers sit up and take notice.

Perhaps the biggest mistake that most other job-hunters make is in ignoring the hidden market that opens up through networking, referrals, recommendations, and word of mouth. These job-hunters sit at home, typing out applications and sending them off. But the people who get all of the plum jobs are the ones who are out and about, buying coffee for friends of friends, having drinks with ex-bosses and ex-colleagues, meeting people and having conversations. The Director of the Career Development Service at a top British business school recently told me that there's a direct relationship between the number of face-to-face conversations you have and how quickly you get a job. So get out there now.

Interviews trip up so many candidates too. Those other candidates think they can get away with rehearsing precise answers to interview questions. But you're going to concentrate on your key strengths, the key skills that you bring that can transfer into greater success for an employer. You will think about not only what you say but how you say it, building rapport and obeying the many unspoken rules that dictate how interviewers like candidates to behave.

Last but not least, you must avoid the pitfall of settling for the wrong job. I have advised scores of people who grumble about the predicament they're in. They moan that the job wasn't what they expected. But you won't. You will get that job offer then invest time in interviewing the employer, finding out exactly what the job entails, what the culture is like, and what your would-be boss is really like.

Follow the rules and you shall get a new job. It really is as simple as that.

ABOUT THE AUTHOR

Rob Yeung is a psychologist and presenter of BBC TV's
How To Get Your Dream Job. A director at leadership
consulting firm Talentspace, he designs assessment
centres and interviews candidates on behalf of
employers.

ALSO BY ROB YEUNG

NETWORKING
THE NEW RULES

- Win friends and allies
- Meet new people with confidence
- Build valuable relationships
- Get people to help you
- Build your profile

Want to get promoted or grow your business?
Want to meet new people with confidence?
Want to build relationships to get ahead?

It's not *what* you know; it's *who* you know. Whether you work for someone else or run your own business, networking will allow you to promote yourself and succeed. Even if you don't know anyone important, this book teaches you how to build a network of people who will fall over themselves to help you reach your goals.

ISBN 978-1-905736-30-0 / £7.99 PAPERBACK

ALSO BY ROB YEUNG

EMOTIONAL INTELLIGENCE
THE NEW RULES

- Motivate yourself
- Boost your confidence
- Enhance your popularity
- Build effective relationships
- Influence people

Want to be more effective and successful?
Want to manage your own moods and emotions?
Want to build more effective relationships?

Emotional intelligence is the skill of managing moods and emotions – in both yourself and other people. Learn to recover from setbacks, motivate yourself, and build personal confidence. Uncover techniques for building effective relationships, dealing with conflict, and becoming more influential. It takes more than brains and hard work to get ahead – and this book tells you how.

ISBN 978-1-905736-29-4 / £7.99 PAPERBACK

ALSO BY ROB YEUNG

ENTREPRENEURSHIP
THE NEW RULES

- Turn your passion into profit
- Create your business concept
- Set up your business
- Find customers and make money
- Grow your business

Thinking about working for yourself?
Want to succeed as an entrepreneur?
Want to grow a profitable business?

Learn the secrets of nurturing a business idea and turning it into a successful and profitable business. Even if you don't yet have a concept for a business, read this book to discover how to find the right seed from which to grow your own business and succeed as an entrepreneur.

ISBN 978-0-462-09927-9 / £7.99 PAPERBACK

ALSO BY ROB YEUNG

OFFICE POLITICS
THE NEW RULES

- Achieve personal and organizational goals
- Influence decision-makers
- Understand political agendas
- Enhance your reputation
- Deal with difficult people

Tired of being overlooked?
Want to enhance your political savvy?
Want to gain support and achieve goals?

The modern workplace is full of backstabbing colleagues, incompetent teammates, and toxic bosses. But office politics can be positive as well as negative. Learn how to defend yourself and get ahead at work – without compromising your values or resorting to underhand tactics.

ISBN 978-0-462-09930-9 / £7.99 PAPERBACK

ALSO BY ROB YEUNG

SHOULD I SLEEP WITH THE BOSS?

And 99 Other Questions about Having a Great Career

Want to get more out of your work? Perhaps you want to get that promotion or pay rise. Maybe you want to feel more motivated about work or want to learn the secrets of achieving more in less time.

Whatever you want from your work, this book is packed with information to help you achieve your career goals. We all know that being smart and good at your job is no longer enough to get ahead. *Should I Sleep with the Boss?* sheds light on exactly what it takes in the modern-day workplace to get paid more, find your motivation, and leave the office on time.

This provocative book provides pithy, informative, and entertaining answers to 100 questions such as: How can I manage my useless boss? How can I escape the ranks of middle management? How can I deflect criticism? How can I learn to say "no"? How can I find my calling in life?

Should I Sleep with the Boss? lays down the rules for success at work in the 21st century. You'll find in this book the answers to the questions you need to be asking. Whatever you want to change or achieve at work, this book will show you how.

ISBN 978-0-462-09922-4 / £9.99 PAPERBACK